BEYOND HAPPINESS AND MEANING

BEYOND HAPPINESS AND MEANING

TRANSFORMING YOUR LIFE THROUGH ETHICAL BEHAVIOR

STEVEN MINTZ

ETHICS SAGE LLC

Beyond Happiness and Meaning:
Transforming Your Life Through Ethical Behavior

Published by Gatekeeper Press
2167 Stringtown Rd, Suite 109
Columbus, OH 43123-2989
www.GatekeeperPress.com

Copyright © 2019 by Steven Mintz

ISBN (paperback): 9781642376296
eISBN: 9781642376302

Printed in the United States of America

Contents

Acknowledgments

I wish to thank my editor, The Artful Editor, for their expert services and timely comments that enhanced the quality of the book. In particular, Christina Palaia went above and beyond the call of duty in editing the book. Her encouragement kept me going throughout the process.

My deepest gratitude goes to Jeremy Dickinson from the Philosophy Department at California State University in San Luis Obispo for his guidance and expert commentary on the philosophy material discussed in the book.

I wish to thank Kara Jensen from Triffid Online Marketing for her insights on marketing the book and website design.

Gatekeeper Press has been invaluable in helping me to navigate the publishing process.

Most of all, I wish to thank the thousands of students I have taught ethics to over the years, who debated the issues with me and lived up to what it means to be ethical people.

Introduction

What is the goal of being human? The goal of life is to achieve happiness and to live a meaningful life. Ethical behavior can get you to those goals. By following the Golden Rule, living a life of virtue, using ethical reasoning, and meeting your moral obligations to others, you can live a happy life filled with meaning.

Most of us want to attain happiness. But what is happiness? How can we achieve it? Why is it important to our well-being? These are key questions to address in the pursuit of happiness. By learning the art of ethical behavior, you can make choices that lead to greater happiness—a feeling that your life is going well.

Most of us also seek greater meaning in our lives. We pursue activities that create a sense of belongingness, build our self-esteem, provide growth opportunities, and guide us on the path to self-fulfillment. By learning the art of ethical behavior, you can develop the skills necessary to make choices in life that enhance meaningful relationships and lead to a life well-lived.

Our friendships, loving relationships, close social relationships, meaningful work experiences, and public relationships developed through social networking provide the scope in which we can practice ethical behavior. The way we treat others influences how they treat us and whether these relationships can bring happiness and greater meaning to our life.

Elizabeth McGrath suggests in *The Art of Ethics*:

> Doing what is ethically right actually uplifts a person and realizes a person's true potential. One becomes invested in doing what is right because it is plainly in their self-interest. . . . Being ethical turns out to be the right thing to do, not only (or even chiefly) because it promotes social stability and order and satisfies the rule makers, but because it makes each actor healthier and more satisfied.[1]

We can pursue happiness and greater meaning in life all by ourselves. However, given the interconnected world we live in, with multiple relationships on different levels, our pursuit would benefit from greater civility in society. Merriam-Webster's dictionary defines *civility* as "polite, reasonable, and respectful behavior." It has been said that "Ethics deals fundamentally with how we treat each other on a daily basis. Indeed, our small acts of civility and incivility constitute the heart of morality."[2]

The premise of this book is that by learning the art of ethical behavior you can transform your life and achieve happiness and greater meaning while reintroducing civility to society. We all stand to gain—more peace, more joy, more happiness, more meaning—when we and others act ethically and with civility.

Though you may not have been born knowing exactly how to act ethically, you can learn with practice and the guidance I supply. Together, we will analyze the resolution of assumed and real-world ethical dilemmas using tried-and-true ethical reasoning methods, and I show you how to make ethical decisions that can bring happiness and greater meaning to your life.

Why You Should Read This Book

Maybe you believe you are an ethical person, so there is no need to read this book. Even so, being ethical is an ongoing commitment to doing the right thing, especially when you are pressured to do otherwise—which seems to so often be the case in our increasingly divided society. Ethical people slip up from time to time, perhaps because they lose sight of what it means to be an ethical person. And some of us have *ethical blind spots*, which are the gaps between who we would like to be and the person we truly are. There is always room to learn more about ethics and how to apply it in the real world.

Maybe, instead, you're wondering, Why be ethical now, when it seems people get further ahead in life by taking the easy way—which is not always the ethical way—out? This may be so, but taking the easy way out doesn't mean you will be happier or gain greater meaning in your life even if you get ahead. Acting in your own interests while harming others doesn't contribute to a life well lived. It may bring happiness, but it's fleeting happiness: the more we get, the more we want, and those who care little about ethics are willing to use others to get their way. Eventually, this backfires because others learn to treat them in the same way.

Ethical behavior is a journey that begins with one step: committing to being an ethical person. Much like the commitments many of us make to lose weight and exercise more, being ethical takes practice and discipline. Like most journeys, it takes time and effort. However, once you learn the tools discussed in this book, you will be able to apply them in everyday life and establish a pattern of ethical behavior that serves you well.

Ethics is a complex subject that encompasses ethical values and standards of behavior that have been debated throughout the course of history. This book will help you understand ethical decision making through a seven-step process: (1) recognizing the ethical issue(s); (2) identifying the ethical values; (3) identifying alternative courses of action; (4) analyzing the ethics of each alternative; (5) deciding on a course of action; (6) checking yourself; and (7) acting ethically. Ethical behavior is the outcome of this process.

This book is designed to have broad appeal, no matter what stage of life you are in. Moral decisions affect us at all ages. Young adults, millennials, middle-age folks, and older people—we can all benefit by learning the art of ethical behavior, applying it to everyday decisions, and doing things that are right, not wrong, and good, not bad, thereby transforming our lives in a way that brings happiness and greater meaning. Young adults and millennials (23-39 years old as of 2019) may find the book particularly appealing because it explains optimal ways to engage on social networking sites, which this group tends to visit on a frequent basis. Folks this age grew up in the social media era, which is generally regarded as starting in 1997, and may be subject to more bouts of incivility than others, so having an ethical decision-making process at hand can help them navigate the sometimes-choppy waters of online behavior.

I have taught ethics as a college professor for over thirty years. I began my career in teaching after completing the Doctor of Business Administration program at the George Washington University. For most of my career, I have taught a course in accounting ethics, using my knowledge of professional ethics gained from working in the accounting profession. Most of the values accountants hold dear are the same that make for an ethical person: honesty, trust, objectivity/fairness, integrity, and responsible behavior.

I first became interested in ethics in the broader sense during the 1970s when issues related to social justice were front and center in the American psyche. The notion that we weren't treating black Americans and other minorities fairly piqued my curiosity as to just what equal treatment and fairness really meant and what I could do to advance the cause of ethics.

One thing I realized early on is not everyone has the same understanding of what it means to be an ethical person. I started to write papers on the topic and made many professional presentations. I have frequently been interviewed for my views on ethical behavior, including most recently by the *New York Times*, which sought me out to share my perspective on the college admissions scandal. I also wrote a book, *Ethical Obligations and Decision Making in Accounting: Text and Cases*, which is now in its fifth edition and used at many colleges and universities.

For the past ten years, I have been writing blog posts under the pseudonym Ethics Sage. My blog has been recognized as one of the best in philosophy and higher education by Feedspot, the content reader for reading all your favorite websites in one place. My workplace ethics advice blog has been recognized as one of the thirty exceptional blogs on corporate social responsibility by Market Inspector, a leading digital marketplace for businesses and institutions in Europe.

I am most proud of being recognized by my peers when I received the Accounting Exemplar Award from the Public Interest Section of the American Accounting Association in 2015. The Public Interest Section addresses broad issues such as the public trust in accounting. I value this award because it validates my work as a teacher and role model for my students.

I hope you will find this book thought-provoking and inspirational and that you commit to being an ethical person. If you do, you will open yourself to happiness and a more self-fulfilling life.

CHAPTER 1

Why Be Ethical

Happiness and moral duty are inseparably connected.

—George Washington

This straightforward quote from the first president of the United States links happiness with our moral obligations to others. Washington explained by saying he is motivated to promote the progress of happiness by practicing moral duty.

Have you ever been out on a few dates, enjoyed them very much, followed up with a text, and then never heard from the other party? If so, you've been *ghosted*. Ghosting occurs when someone you believe cares about you, such as a person you have been dating, disappears from contact without any explanation at all—no phone call, email, or text.[3] Ghosting also occurs when a candidate for a job opening interviews with a firm, receives a job offer, but doesn't respond. They just seem to disappear.

Consider the following situation: Sally has gone out on two dates with Bill, a guy she met online. Bill clearly cares about Sally. However, Sally doesn't share those feelings. After the second date, Sally decides the relationship isn't going anywhere, so she starts ignoring phone calls and texts from Bill. However, she wonders whether she should contact Bill and tell him about her decision. Does Sally have a moral duty to inform Bill? More will be said about this later in the chapter.

If you were Sally, how would you know how to act? What's the right thing to do? It can be confusing or uncomfortable, but with ethics you can wade through these situations and feel good about yourself by behaving rightly. To do so, you need to understand what ethics is.

Ethics is about the choices we make and the reasons we make them. A simple definition of ethics is the principles of behavior that help us distinguish good from bad, right from wrong. Our choices are a function of our beliefs and values. Our reasons for the way we act are the motivations we have and what we intend the outcome to be.

We use ethics—whether we realize it or not—to evaluate and decide among competing options in everyday situations.[4] We face ethical decisions all the time, so it is important to ask: How should I decide what to do and why? The ethical decision-making process described in this book answers that question.

Branches of Ethics

Ethical philosophies—that is, theories of right and wrong behavior—can be thought of in a broad sense as normative, descriptive, or applied ethics. *Normative ethics* addresses "how things should or ought to be, how to value them, which things are good or bad, and which actions are right or wrong. It attempts to develop a set of rules governing human conduct, or a set of norms for action."[5] Normative ethics is emphasized in this book.

Descriptive theories consider ethics by observing actual choices people make. *Descriptive ethics* sounds like its name and describes ethics from the point of view of how things have occurred and why; it is not prescriptive in describing how ethics *should be* practiced. As such, because these theories are simply observational and descriptive, they do not provide the kind of guidance we need to evaluate ethical dilemmas and reason an ethical course of action to take.

Applied ethics is also what its name sounds like: we apply moral reasoning to practical situations. We can use the theories and conclusions of normative ethics to evaluate real-life moral problems and resolve them through applied ethics. For example, should we ghost a person we no longer date who is persistent and wants to know the reason we broke it off? We can consider this dilemma in light of normative ethics and then apply our moral reasoning in real life.

The Golden Rule

A universal principle of moral behavior is the *Golden Rule.* It says: Do unto others as you would have them do unto you. Simply stated, we should treat others the way we wish to be treated. The Golden Rule is considered a *universal* moral principle because, in one form or another, it has been esteemed and appreciated across cultures and since ancient times (as discussed below).

The Golden Rule is the underlying tenet of morality in most religions and cultures around the world and serves as a guideline for ethical behavior. Table 1.1 shows how this principle has been incorporated into religious writings.

Table 1.1
The Universality of the Golden Rule in World Religions

Religion	Expression of the Golden Rule	Citation
Christianity	All things whatsoever ye would that men should do to you, Do ye so to them; for this is the law and the prophets.	Matthew 7:1
Confucianism	Do not do to others what you would not like yourself. Then there will be no resentment against you, either in the family or in the state.	Analects 12:2
Buddhism	Hurt not others in ways that you yourself would find hurtful.	Uda-Navarga 5,1
Hinduism	This is the sum of duty, do naught onto others what you would not have them do unto you.	Mahabharata 5, 1517
Islam	No one of you is a believer until he desires for his brother that which he desires for himself.	Sunnah
Judaism	What is hateful to you, do not do to your fellowman. This is the entire Law; all the rest is commentary.	Talmud, Shabbat 3id
Taoism	Regard your neighbor's gain as your gain, and your neighbor's loss as your own loss.	Tai Shang Kan Yin P'ien
Zoroastrianism	That nature alone is good which refrains from doing to another whatsoever is not good for itself.	Dadisten-I-dinik, 94, 5

Some have described the Golden Rule as an ethic of reciprocity in that we should treat others with the same consideration that we demand for ourselves.[6] Treating others as we would want to be treated inspires us to treat them with respect, kindness, and fairness.

Others have been more definitive and interpret the Golden Rule as "treat others only as you consent to be treated in the same situation." Here, we must imagine ourselves on the receiving end of the action in the exact place of the other person, even with their likes and dislikes. If we act in a given way toward another, and yet are unwilling to be treated that way in the same circumstances, then we violate the rule.[7]

For example, let's assume you are a manager and must choose between two employees for a promotion. The first employee is the higher performer, yet you like the second more. If you choose the second employee but would want the promotion for yourself had you been in the same position as the first, then you have violated the rule. Here, we could say, that we should treat others the way we wish they would treat us.

The Golden Rule is best seen as a consistency principle. It doesn't replace the ethical principles that prescribe behavior and that are used in ethical reasoning, as discussed in this book. It isn't an infallible guide to which actions are right or wrong. It doesn't have all the answers. But it aligns our actions toward others with our desires if the situation were reversed.[8] However, it doesn't tell us what to do when our desired action doesn't match what the other person would want to happen.

Consider the following: You want your aging mother to live with you in her remaining years. You believe it's the responsibility of a son or daughter to take care of an aging parent, and this is the way you would want to be treated when you are older, but she refuses. She wants to be independent, to live in the house she grew up in, and she doesn't want to impose on you. Do you respect her desire for independence and treat her the way *she* wants or pressure her to move in with you, which is what *you* would prefer and feel is best for her? The Golden Rule doesn't work well here, and another approach might be better, such as to weigh the good and the bad of each alternative. The aging parent example is discussed in full in Chapter 5.

The Golden Rule prescribes how we should treat others but doesn't always describe what a person will do. This depends on the character of each individual and the circumstances encountered.

An interesting observation comes from the American author and philosopher Aldo Leopold: "Ethical behavior is doing the right thing when no one else is watching—even when doing the wrong thing is legal." Most people act ethically when they know they are being watched. But, once there is a separation between the actor and the affected party or parties, self-serving motivations may play a greater role in behavior.

For example, someone who sees another person drop a $5 bill is more likely to pocket the money if the one who dropped it is unaware. Even though it's legal to keep the money, an ethical person would give it back because it is the right thing to do. What if you had dropped the money? Wouldn't you want it returned?

What if it was $50? Some might say (if they are being honest) that they would keep it because it's a lot of money. However, there is no materiality test with ethics. The Golden Rule here is "Never steal from another" because presumably we would want lost money returned to us if we were in that situation. So, if it's wrong to keep someone else's money, it's wrong regardless of the amount.

Normative Ethical Theories

Normative ethics, one of the main branches of ethics and the branch this book mainly deals with, is usually itself split into three main categories: virtue ethics, deontology (the study of moral obligation or duty), and teleology (consequentialist theory, judging actions by their results or consequences). Table 1.2 provides a summary of the normative ethical theories. You can refer to it during the discussions about ethical decision making that follow.

Table 1.2 Normative Ethical Theories

CLASSICAL GREEK PHILOSOPHIES			
Philosophical Method	Proponents	Ethical Principle	Basis for Ethical Decision Making
Virtue Ethics	Aristotle, Plato, Socrates	Develop moral and intellectual virtues	Seek human excellence through a life of virtue
MODERN PHILOSOPHIES			
Deontology		Categorical Imperative	
(Rights Theory)	Immanuel Kant	Formula of Humanity	Respect the rights of others to choose for themselves
(Duties)		Formula of Universality	Satisfy duties to oneself and others

Teleology Egoism			
(Ethical)	Henry Sidgwick	Maximize individual pleasure	Promote one's own good
(Rational)	Ayn Rand	Virtue of rationality	Promote one's own interests in accordance with reason
(Enlightened)	Alexis de Tocqueville	Self-interest rightly understood	Allow for the well-being of others in pursuing one's own interest
Teleology Utilitarianism			
(Act Utilitarianism)	John Stuart Mill / Jeremy Bentham	Greatest Happiness Principle	Choose the act that produces best consequences for oneself and others
(Rule Utilitarianism)	John Stuart Mill		Choose the act that conforms to the general rule that produces the best consequences

Virtue Ethics

The classical Greek philosophy of virtue espoused by Socrates, Plato, and Aristotle deals with the question: What is the best sort of life for human beings to live? Greek thinkers saw the attainment of a good life as the end, or goal, of human existence. As human beings, we have certain aims and goals in life toward which our actions are directed. Our end goal is a state of happiness or human flourishing. The ultimate end is to live a life of happiness through the exercise of virtue.[9] For more on the ancient Greek philosophers, see Exhibit 1.1.

Exhibit 1.1

Ancient Greek Philosophers

Greek philosophy arose in the sixth century BCE and lasted for hundreds of years, although its influence continues to this day through the process of logically and methodologically thinking through life's big questions.[10] The three best-known philosophers, Socrates, Plato, and Aristotle, contributed to the philosophy in a significant way. Greek philosophy has had a major influence on Western thought.

Socrates is credited as one of the founders of Western philosophy. His largest contribution is the Socratic method, a form of inquiry and discussion based on asking and answering questions to illuminate ideas. Socrates wrote nothing himself. What we know of him comes from the writings of Plato, who recorded the dialogues between the two.

Aristotle was Plato's best student. A key theme of his thought is that happiness is the goal of life. The founder of logical theory, Aristotle believed that the greatest human endeavor is the use of reason in theoretical activity.[11]

Aristotle's most popular work on virtue ethics is *Nicomachean Ethics*. The virtues he lists in the book fall into two categories: moral virtues and intellectual virtues. *Moral virtues* govern our behavior and include such traits as generosity, friendliness or courtesy, truthfulness, patience (moderation in action), temperance or self-control, courage, and justice. Moral virtues are learned by performing virtuous acts, like being courageous. *Intellectual virtues* (our thought process, broadly stated) are acquired through understanding, good judgment, reasoning abilities, and practical wisdom; they govern ethical behavior and are expressed in purposeful action and contemplation. Intellectual virtues are gained through deliberation about what is right to do.

A *virtue* is a trait or quality that is deemed morally good. The general concept behind virtue ethics is that a person with a moral character embodies admirable traits that individuals should choose to guide their personal behavior. These character traits, such as the Six Pillars (discussed below), become part of a person's virtuous character with practice and repetition. Rather than relying on external standards such as universal laws or philosophical standards of ethical reasoning, virtue ethics relies on developing excellences of character to guide behavior. These excellences become the motivating factors for a person's choices and actions.

In virtue ethics, *character* is a state of being that lies between two extremes of behavior, one of excess or going too far, and the other of deficiency or not going far enough. For example, assume an individual commits a crime and could be punished with an extremely harsh penalty or let off lightly. These are the extremes of justice: one sentence is unfair while the other overly fair. A just sentence is somewhere in between.

Aristotle conceived of the middle ground as the *Golden Mean*, an idea in virtue theory that extremes in behavior should be avoided and, instead, moderation of one's actions would lead to virtuous behavior.[12] For example, he considered self-control a virtue because it enables a person to moderate their behavior, in particular their emotions, desires, or the expression of them, in the choices they make. Self-control requires a strong will to self-regulate behavior. It's not easy, but we can incorporate the virtue of self-control into our character by avoiding excessive behaviors that can be harmful to ourselves or others and by practicing good judgment about our choices.

For example, narcotic pain medications like opioids increasingly have been prescribed to treat chronic pain that results from a variety of ailments, including cancer, back surgery, or osteoarthritis. Taking too much of these medications can lead to physical dependence and addiction, whereas using too little may not treat the pain adequately and might lead to a desire for stronger opioids such as fentanyl, which, in its intravenous form, is seventy to a hundred times more potent than morphine. A person who possesses the virtue of self-control is able to regulate their intake of opioids and take them only when absolutely necessary and in prescribed doses.

Aristotle believed that our proper function consists in reasoning and acting in accord with reason, as in the case of opioid use. This is the heart of the doctrine of virtue ethics: We deliberate about things that are within our power and that can we can realize in action. We deliberate about the means to ends (i.e., virtues) and the end itself—human flourishing. We make choices to achieve that end.

The end goal of exercising virtue is to bring happiness and meaning to life. A happy life fulfills a broad range of conditions, including physical and mental well-being.[13] A meaningful life has purpose and is one worth living. It follows that the possession and exercise of moral and intellectual virtues are essential to our well-being. They represent the inner qualities that form the basis of a life well lived.

The presence of moral virtues, then, can direct a person's

behavior to achieve moral excellence and a state of *eudaimonia*, the Greek word for "happiness" or "welfare," the highest human good. However, the Greeks thought of happiness in broader terms, linking it to moral excellence and the end state of human flourishing. *Human flourishing* is characterized by a life worth living, the good life, and a state of well-being. A life worth living is one in which meaning is realized through our actions, which are guided by intellectual virtues, including the ability to deliberate about the proper course of action and apply knowledge to each situation encountered.[14]

The following illustrates these relationships and the link to happiness and meaning:

Starting point →	Exercise virtue →	Pursue moral excellence →	Achieve end goal of life: Well-being
Understand virtues (the excellences of character)	Develop moral and intellectual virtues	Achieve moral excellence through practice of virtues	Realize happiness (human flourishing) and meaning (self-actualization) through moral excellence

In writing about moral philosophy, Richard Burner and Yvonne Raley state: "A person must fulfill several conditions to count as having attained moral excellence:

1. They must know what the right thing to do is.

2. They must intend to do the right thing because it is the right thing to do.

3. Their right actions must be the products of their own firm and unchangeable character—behavioral patterns must be habitual or second nature.

For example, what makes the virtue of courage an excellence of character is more than practicing courage. We must also know what courage is, intend to act courageously because it is good to do so, and courage must be part of our enduring character traits."[15]

Imagine your best friend and coworker pads his expense account on out-of-town work trips. You've spoken to him about it. He knows it violates company policy but does it anyway because the accountant is lax with enforcing the rules. You know it's wrong and don't want to get your friend in trouble. Still, you report the matter to a supervisor because you don't want to be part of a cover-up. This is an act of courage in which your motivation for action is to do the right thing because it is the right thing to do even if there are personal costs. If you repeat such courageous actions in other situations, then it can become a consistent part of your behavior, an excellence of character, and virtuous.

Some virtues may conflict. Acting courageously, for example, has its limitations. We probably shouldn't fight back against a mugger who brandishes a gun while taking our money. It may be the courageous thing to do but also can get us hurt or killed. Acting cautiously instead, which reflects the virtue of self-control, probably is the better choice.

Conflicts between virtues can be resolved through ethical reasoning. For example, can empathy for a friend's situation ever require you to be dishonest? What if a criminal is after your friend because she testified against him at his trial? He's out of prison and wants revenge. Most of us would put empathy over honesty and lie to the criminal about our friend's whereabouts because we are concerned for their well-being. In this situation, we would reason that we have a moral duty to protect life and limb.

The Six Pillars of Character

Ethical values underlie the Golden Rule and combine to create a person's virtuous character. These values describe what it means to treat others as we would wish to be treated. We can think of the ethical values as a bridge between the Golden Rule and the philosophical standards of behavior that apply to ethical reasoning discussed later.

Golden Rule	Ethical Values	Ethical Reasoning
Treat others the way we wish they would treat us	Ways we should wish to be treated (i.e., kindness, respect)	How we should act to resolve ethical dilemmas about the best way to treat others

The Josephson Institute of Ethics provides a set of ethical values that reflect praiseworthy traits of character called the *Six Pillars of Character*. According to the founder, Michael Josephson, "To say a person has a good character or even to admire a person's character does not require that they be perfect but it does mean we think this is a good person worthy of trust and admiration."[16] Exhibit 1.2 provides some background information on the Josephson Institute.

Exhibit 1.2

The Josephson Institute of Ethics

The Josephson Institute was founded in 1987. Its purpose is to increase ethical commitment, competence, and practice in all segments of society. The institute does this through its Character Counts program, which teaches a shared language and framework of values called the Six Pillars of Character. These programs reach about eight million young people and their families each year. Every year since 1993, the U.S. Senate has passed a joint resolution and the president has signed a proclamation declaring the third week in October National Character Counts Week.[17]

The Six Pillars of Character form the basis for a set of beliefs that can be thought of in terms of moral duties and virtues that flow from six core ethical values. Josephson believes that the Six Pillars can dramatically improve the ethical quality of our decisions, and thus our character and our life. Acting on these values opens up the possibility that we can build meaningful relationships that bring happiness and contentment, thereby enhancing well-being.

The Six Pillars include trustworthiness, respect, responsibility, fairness, caring, and citizenship. What follows is a brief description of each as described in Josephson's *Making Ethical Decisions*.[18]

I've added explanations to show the link between ethical values and happiness and meaning.

Trustworthiness

Trustworthiness means living up to the expectations of others and refraining from telling even small lies or behaving in a self-serving fashion that can destroy relationships. When others trust us, they believe we will live up to our obligations and don't need to be monitored. They hold us in higher esteem. They value us for who we are and what we do, and that adds meaning to our life.

Being trustworthy means to follow up on our words with action. This occurs by behaving in certain ways, including exhibiting the following characteristic traits of good behavior:

Honesty. Expressing the truth (facts) as best we know it and not conveying it in a way likely to mislead or deceive. Honesty in conduct is playing by the rules, without stealing, cheating, fraud, and other trickery.

Integrity. Acting according to one's beliefs, not according to expediency. Acting consistently from situation to situation.

Reliability (Promise Keeping). Keeping promises and honoring commitments to others by accepting the responsibility of making all reasonable efforts to fulfill commitments.

Loyalty. Creating an expectation of allegiance, fidelity, and devotion. The responsibility to promote the interests of other people and organizations. A duty that goes beyond the normal obligation we all share to care for others. A more complete definition of loyalty that recognizes rightful behavior is being faithful to our obligations to others to promote their interests but in a way that doesn't harm others.

Respect

Respect is treating people with dignity, courtesy, decency, autonomy, tolerance, and acceptance. Merriam-Webster's online dictionary links *respect* to holding someone in high regard or esteem. Although we have no ethical duty to hold people in high esteem, we should treat everyone with a basic level of respect because it's the foundation of civility.

We have a responsibility to be the best we can be when dealing with others even if they are unpleasant people or we disagree with their message. Josephson points out that respect fits nicely into the Golden Rule because we should want others to be respectful toward us, so we should do the same in our treatment of them.

Responsibility (Promise Keeping)

Responsible means being accountable for the choices we make in life. We recognize that our actions matter and that we are answerable for the consequences of our behavior.

A responsible person plans ahead, is diligent, perseveres, does their best, exercises self-discipline and self-control, and thinks before they act. We can equate these characteristics with the exercise of moral and intellectual virtues.

Responsible behavior builds character because we keep our promises, honor our commitments, and pursue excellence in whatever we do. We act this way to gain the trust of others and develop meaningful relationships. Acting responsibly is an important component of a life well lived.

Fairness

Fairness is a subjective concept but typically involves issues of equality, impartiality, and due process. Fairness implies adherence to a balanced standard of justice without relevance to one's own feelings or inclinations. The absence of bias is the essence of fairness. For example, treating others differently because of their race, religion, national origin, sex, or sexual preference is wrong because it singles out one group for different treatment, not based on the character of their actions or words but simply because they are different.

In a study of well-being in the United States, researchers questioned fifty thousand respondents about their levels of happiness along with their perceptions of how fair and trustworthy other people are. The results indicate that "a sense of fairness and trust are associated with happiness perhaps because they are a building block of social relationships and community . . . and having satisfying social relationships is important [to happiness.]"[19]

Caring

Caring is identified in the Six Pillars as being the heart of ethics and ethical decision making. As Josephson points out, we can't be "truly ethical and yet be unconcerned with the welfare of others. That is because ethics is ultimately about good relations with other people." Caring people treat others kindly and with compassion. Caring people do not treat others as instruments of their will. Instead, they treat people, indeed all of humanity, as ends in themselves with intrinsic value: people are valuable and we should care about them simply because they are members of humanity.

A person who is compassionate is concerned about the condition of others and feels an emotional response to both their pain and pleasure. They are empathetic.

Compassion for others can bring tangible benefits. Research has shown that during periods of stress and sadness we focus too much on what's wrong with our lives and not enough on helping others in need. Turning our attention outward as caring behavior can make us feel better about ourselves and gain some perspective on our own situation. Helping others can be contagious—acts of generosity and kindness beget more generosity in a chain reaction of goodness. Happiness spreads and if people around us are happy we, in turn, become happier as well.[20]

Citizenship

Citizenship includes civic virtues and duties that prescribe how we ought to behave as part of a community. It means being a positive force for others. Obeying laws, paying taxes, voting, and being charitable are ways good citizens can benefit others in their community and improve the well-being of everyone.

Civility is a civic virtue that calls us to look inward and assess whether we are treating others in our community with understanding, respect, and fairness. As such, civility is an essential element of acting in accordance with the Golden Rule.

If we could wave a magic wand and bring greater civility to society, I believe we all would benefit by gaining more peace and contentment. Acts of incivility are the antithesis of ethical behavior. All too often we watch as one group shouts down another, makes disparaging remarks about someone else, gets in the face of an opponent, and even promotes violence. These kinds of behaviors have no place in a civil society. We all need to learn how to disagree without being disagreeable.

Deontology

Theories of deontology, one of the three forms of ethics on the main branch of normative ethics, emphasize the universal ethical principles that should be followed irrespective of the outcomes or consequences on the actor. One such principle might be "never lie"; another, "never steal." These are examples of *unconditional* moral obligations that are binding in all situations without regard to the consequences of those actions.

Deontological ethics, or duty ethics, as it is also known, bases morality on foundational principles of obligation. Unlike in teleology, where the morality of lying or stealing would be evaluated on the basis of the consequences of such an act, in deontology moral responses are fixed and invariable. For example, it's *always* wrong to steal from another even if one's family is starving for food. Deontology makes no exceptions and can be an unforgiving method of ethical reasoning.

One duty-based, deontological approach to ethics is rights theory. A *right* is a justified claim against another person. For example, I have a *right* to keep that which is mine (i.e., I earned it through hard work or fortune) so that others have a *duty* not to do anything to take it away from me.

Theories of rights can be traced back to the philosopher John Locke (1632–1704) and are the basis for the inalienable (natural, nonnegotiable, and nontransferable) rights to life, liberty, and the pursuit of happiness discussed in the United States Declaration of Independence. Locke believed that the pursuit of happiness was the highest good and the end of human action.[21]

One of the most important interpretations of moral rights and duties is based on the work of Immanuel Kant (1724–1804). Kant believed that one's intentions/reasons/motivations for acting are the bases for moral action. Our motive for acting should be to meet our moral duties to others.

An important part of Kant's theory is the concept of good will. His influential work on the philosophy of ethics, *The Groundwork for the Metaphysics of Morals* (*Groundwork*),

begins by saying: "Nothing can possibly be conceived in the
world, or even out of it, which can be called good without
qualification, except a good will." In order for something to be
good "without qualification," it must be "good" as a means to
an end but also "bad" as a means to some other end. Kant's
point is that to be universally and absolutely good, something
must be good in every instance of its occurrence.[22]

The good will freely chooses to do its moral duty, according
to Kant. That duty, in turn, is motivated solely by reason.
Because the dictates of reason allow for no exceptions, moral
duty is absolute.

In *Groundwork*, Kant applied a *categorical imperative* to
determine the moral validity for a particular action. It is categorical because it is not dependent on a person's inclination
or purpose. It is an imperative because it is an unconditional
moral obligation.

According to Kant, each of us has a worth or dignity that
must be respected. This dignity makes it wrong for others to
abuse us or to use us against our will. There are two forms of
the categorical imperative; one is the *formula of humanity*:
humanity must always be treated as an end, not merely a means.
To treat someone as a mere means, or to use someone merely
to advance one's own interests, as might be rationalized under
egoism (discussed next), is wrong. To treat a person as an end
is to respect that person's dignity by allowing him or her the
freedom to make their own choices.[23]

In other words, as individuals, we all have natural rights
that include autonomy, self-determination, and freedom.

The most well-known form of the categorical imperative is
the *formula of universal law*. The formula of universal law is
Kant's famous statement of duty: "Act only according to that
maxim by which you can at the same time will that it should
become a universal law." The "maxim" of our acts can be thought

of as the reason behind our acts. This version establishes that our reasons need to be universal.[24]

Essentially, we should act only in a way that we would want the maxim (reason for acting) to become a universal law that, because the reason is rational, everyone would follow and act in precisely the same way.[25]

At first glance it may seem that the universality principle of the categorical imperative makes it similar to the Golden Rule. However, there is one big difference. The Golden Rule says we should act toward others the way we wish they would act toward us. In other words, we must ask ourselves how we feel about what is done toward us and strive to treat others in a way that we would favor. The problem is we may have a different interpretation of what we would want if we were in the other person's position. Perhaps we lie to others because we don't mind being lied to, but another person values truthfulness above all else, so our treatment of them according to the Golden Rule causes trouble.

Kant's universal perspective takes the view of a rational agent, or a decision maker who chooses based on reason. Presumably, a rational agent would not want others to lie all the time (universally) because all trust would vanish and decisions would be made on the basis of false information. Therefore, we cannot will others to lie because of its disruptive force. Moreover, people are ends in themselves, so we have to pay attention to what they want.

In comparison to the principle of utility which forms the basis for consequentialism (discussed below) and where outcomes in the form of happiness are the basis for decisions, the categorical imperative looks at whether a possible action fulfills our duty to society by evaluating its universality. An action is right if it can be universalized into an action everyone could follow without conflict, and it is wrong if it cannot.

Kant addressed virtue in the context of duty and happiness. He conceived of virtue as the strength or will to fulfill one's duties despite any opposing inclinations. He believed that to be fully virtuous is to have a good will that is ready to overcome temptations to immorality. Although we can never fully achieve it, we have a duty to strive for it. Virtue is the supreme and unconditioned good (moral good), and happiness is the conditioned good (effect of virtuous behavior).

Although Kant dismisses the notion of the pursuit of happiness as an end goal in life, he does recognize its relevance to satisfying our duties to others through the formulations of the categorical imperative. He recognizes that sometimes happiness and duty coincide, but it is vital to act from duty alone by ignoring the pull of our inclinations. If our happiness conflicts with our duties to others, then happiness must be set aside. For example, assume you found out that your best friend started a GoFundMe campaign, claiming to be dying of cancer and needing money for lifesaving treatment, none of which is true. He raised $200,000 in two weeks. Would you inform the authorities of the fraud? You have a moral obligation to do so because others have been scammed, and surely you wouldn't want everyone to act in the same way as your friend. Still, you probably won't be happy sending your best friend to jail.

Teleology

In teleology, the rightness or wrongness of actions is based solely on the goodness or badness of their consequences. Theories of teleology are also called *consequentialist theories*, those that base moral judgments on the outcomes of a decision or action, not the motives or intentions in forming the decision. The judgment of right or wrong depends on the consequences of the decision or action for oneself and for others. The two main consequentialist theories considered in this section are egoism and utilitarianism.

Egoism

Egoism is the theory that one's self-interest is, or should be, the motivation for all actions. Right behavior is defined in terms of its consequences for the individual decision maker. Egoists believe that decisions should be made to maximize one's own self-interest, which each individual defines differently. Simply stated, an egoist should "do the act that promotes the greatest good for oneself."[26]

There are a variety of versions of egoism. The ones discussed here are ethical egoism, rational egoism, and enlightened egoism. Each addresses how one's own self-interest relates to satisfying the interests of others.

Ethical Egoism

Ethical egoism was introduced by the philosopher Henry Sidgwick (1838–1900) in 1874 in his book *The Methods of Ethics*. Sidgwick compared egoism to the philosophy of utilitarianism (discussed below), writing that whereas utilitarianism sought to maximize overall pleasure, egoism focused on maximizing only individual pleasure.[27]

As a brand of egoism, ethical egoism claims that the promotion of one's own good is in accordance with morality and that personal happiness is intrinsically valuable insofar as it is pursued for its own sake and not for any other reason. In complying with ethical egoism, individuals aim to promote their own greatest good, and no one has any obligation to promote anyone else's interests.[28]

Philosophers point to some problems with ethical egoism. First, the ethical egoist would not want ethical egoism to be universalized. If it were universalized, others would be deterred from acting altruistically toward anyone, the egoist included, which would be against the egoist's self-interests.

Second, ethical egoism offers no means of resolving conflicts of interest. For example, a company wants to empty toxic waste into a river; the people living downstream object. Ethical egoism simply advises both parties to the conflict to actively pursue their own interests and what they want. In that way, it cannot suggest any sort of resolution or commonsense compromise.[29]

Last, ethical egoism goes against the principle of impartiality because each individual gives themselves preferential treatment in pursuing their own interests without regard to how it affects others.

Rational Egoism

Rational egoism is another brand of egoism that claims the promotion of one's own interests is rational and always in accordance with reason; in other words, an action is rational if and only if it maximizes one's self-interest. One of the most well-known proponents of rational egoism was the contemporary philosopher Ayn Rand (1905–1982).

Rand's philosophy of rational individualism has been called *objectivism*. It's a complicated theory but can be boiled down to an ethics of choice, guided by reason, with no greater moral goal than achieving happiness. As humans, we choose our values; they do not come to us automatically. A proper morality is not about categorical imperatives or duties. Instead, it's about what we want in life and what we must do to get it.[30]

According to Douglas Rasmussen writing in the *Journal of Ayn Rand Studies:* "What determines whether an action ought to be taken depends on whether it will attain the goal chosen by the person. There can be no such thing as doing something from a motive of duty, that is, simply because one ought to."[31]

For Rand, in order to live and prosper, we must uphold and employ the one fundamental value that makes identifying and pursuing all our other values possible: reason. She conceived of reason as the basic virtue and source of all other virtues. The virtue of rationality means the recognition and acceptance of reason as one's only source of knowledge, one's only judge of values, and one's only guide to action.[32]

In rational egoism, individuals are treated as ends in themselves—the ultimate value in life—not the means to the ends of others. If it is true that the pursuit of self-interest is the rational basis for decision making and coincides with happiness, then it may seem that acting in the interests of others can never bring true happiness. If that is the case, then the sacrifices individuals make to improve the lives of others that do not create happiness for the decision maker never make sense.

Enlightened Egoism

One method of egoism that does recognize the interests of others is *enlightened egoism*. It emphasizes more of a direct action to bring about the best interests of society. Enlightened self-interest was discussed by Alexis de Tocqueville (1805–1859) in his work *Democracy in America*. He believed that Americans voluntarily join together in associations to further the interests of the group and, thereby, to serve their own interests. He used "self-interest rightly understood" to describe this concept.[33]

In other words, enlightened egoism is advocated as a means rather than an end, based on the belief that if everyone were to pursue their own interests, general prosperity would be maximized.

Enlightened egoism is the idea that doing what is good for yourself is also doing what is good for others, and vice versa. Enlightened self-interest poses the question of whether it is to the advantage of a person to work for the good of all. As a form of egoism, it allows for accommodating the well-being of others when that helps achieve some ultimate goal of the decision maker, although the decision maker's own self-interest remains paramount.

A concern about enlightened egoism is that it might lead to using others to accomplish one's own goals and then rationalizing that the action was in the best interests of others. The company dumping toxic waste into the river might reason that that act is less expensive than cleaning it up, which saves the company money and allows it to continue employment at the same level, which benefits employees and the community. Weighing these benefits and the related costs, as is done through utilitarianism (discussed next), provides an ethically more responsible approach.

Egoism, in all its forms, highlights the importance of pursuing self-interests, but that's a given in all the ethical reasoning methods. What's most important is how we define "best interest." Is it to maximize the good for all while minimizing the bad (utilitarianism)? Or do we strive to satisfy our moral duties to others and in that way serve our own best interest and those of others (deontology)? In each case, the interests of others are taken into consideration.

The pursuit of happiness and meaning brings us in contact with others, and relationships should allow us to act in the best interests of others, especially when it brings happiness and meaning to us. Given the drawbacks, ethically, of focusing solely on self-interest, the discussions that follow in the book emphasize enlightened egoism because it is a counterpoint to pure egoism.

Utilitarianism

Utilitarianism is a form of consequentialism (teleology), the idea that the morality of an action is judged solely by its consequences. As a moral theory, utilitarianism holds that the best action is the one that maximizes utility. *Utility* is defined in various ways, usually in terms of the well-being of all sentient beings. An action is morally right or justifiable if its contribution to humanity is positive. More specifically, the principle of utility is the teleological concept that states: "Actions or behaviors are right in so far as they promote happiness or pleasure, wrong as they tend to produce unhappiness or pain."[34]

Happiness is an important part of utilitarianism. Utility is found in everything that contributes to the happiness of every rational being. The criterion of good or bad is balanced between an individual's happiness and the happiness of communities or societies. The principle of utility has sometimes been referred to as the *Greatest Happiness Principle*. Under the Greatest Happiness Principle, actions are considered moral when they promote happiness and avoid unhappiness. The optimal choice of action is that which maximizes pleasure over pain.

As an ethical reasoning method, utilitarianism seeks to provide an answer to the practical question "What ought a person to do?" Its answer is that one should act so as to produce the best consequences possible: an action is morally right if its consequences lead to happiness and wrong if it ends in unhappiness. Happiness, which forms the utilitarian standard of what is right conduct, does not refer to the decision maker's own happiness but the happiness of all concerned. We should always act to maximize happiness for all.[35]

One of the foremost utilitarian theorists was Jeremy Bentham (1748–1832). Bentham described benefits and harms in terms of pleasure and pain. He linked them to utility in this way: universal conformity to the principle of utility ("Act always so as to maximize total net balance of pleasures and pains") would maximize the good of society.[36]

By the "good of society," Bentham meant an action should promote the overall happiness of society.

John Stuart Mill (1806–1873), a British philosopher, modified the philosophy of utility by focusing on maximizing the general happiness. According to his view of utilitarianism, actions are in the right proportion when they tend to promote happiness, wrong when they tend to promote unhappiness. Happiness should be promoted to the greatest extent possible.[37]

This means that the decision that produces more happiness than unhappiness for all concerned is good and ethical.

Utilitarianism has found a captive audience in modern times because of its emphasis on cost-benefit tradeoffs. An action is not right or wrong based on duties to others. Instead, right or wrong depends on consequences that are, at least theoretically, measurable outcomes. The challenge is to identify all of these consequences, present and future, and assign a value to them. This is the essence of ethical dilemmas in business when one company's product allegedly has a defect or causes harmful effects and the business must determine whether it costs more to fix the problem than any benefits derived thereby. More is said about these kinds of issues in Chapter 4.

Modern-day utilitarians divide themselves roughly into two groups: act utilitarians and rule utilitarians. An *act utilitarian* believes the principle of utility should be applied to individual acts. Thus, one measures consequences of each individual action according to whether it maximizes good. A *rule utilitarian*, on the other hand, believes that instead of considering results of specific actions, one must weigh the consequences of adopting a general rule exemplified by that action and then judge individual actions by seeing if they conform to those rules whose acceptance produces the most utility.[38]

There is some controversy over whether Mill was, at least in part, a proponent of rule utilitarianism. By one account, he was a proponent because of the statement "that an act is correct when it corresponds to rules whose preservation increases the mass of happiness in the world." Thus, he recognized the importance of rules when they promote the greatest happiness.[39]

One problem with utilitarianism is the difficulty of knowing what will maximize overall happiness. How can we determine the possible effects and which people, present and future, will be affected by each of the actions we might perform?[40]

Moreover, the principle allows for inflicting pain so long as the majority of people are happier. So, we might ask is torture acceptable if the benefits to society are greater than the negative consequences being inflicted on the individual? This might occur if the information gained by torturing someone provides more benefits to society than harms. Under act utilitarianism it would seem so, but under rule utilitarianism (discussed below), it would be wrong to violate the rule that torture is always bad regardless of its utilitarian benefits.

Another problem with act utilitarianism is that it may be used to rationalize otherwise unethical actions by claiming the good outweighs the bad, even though the bad is substantial. Take cheating on exams: An act utilitarian would consider the possible benefits of cheating (a higher grade point average, better job, more pay) and weigh them against the harms (getting caught, being suspended, losing the opportunity to learn material). The act utilitarian might conclude the potential benefits of cheating outweigh the harms.

Rule utilitarians, on the other hand, claim that we must choose the action that conforms to the general rule that would have the best consequences. For the rule utilitarian, actions are justified by appealing to rules such as "don't cheat." The reasoning might go something like this: if everyone cheated, grades would mean nothing (although some students might do a better job at cheating than others), teachers would not know which topics they should spend more time on, unqualified students might graduate with honors, employers might hire the wrong candidates, the university's reputation might be tainted.

The rule utilitarian would claim that we can't break the general rule "don't cheat" even if doing so in a particular circumstance leads to more overall happiness. This is because, in the long run, violating this rule—like violating moral rules in general—leads to more unhappiness. Thus, rule utilitarianism is more closely aligned with deontology than any of the other ethical reasoning methods.

Other Ethical Reasoning Methods

Virtue ethics, deontology, and teleology are normative methods of ethical reasoning that focus on what is moral. They prescribe ways in which we should act. These practices are incorporated into Table 1.2 (see p. 13), which summarizes thought processes used in this book to resolve ethical dilemmas. Two additional methods are discussed below: justice and moral nihilism.

Theories of *justice* deal with how to distribute benefits and burdens in society, but justice is best thought of as a virtue in this book. Justice issues are considered insomuch as we should treat others fairly, so justice is a virtue that supports the Golden Rule.

Friedrich Nietzsche (1844–1900) was a German philosopher who conceptualized *moral nihilism*, the meta-ethical view that nothing is intrinsically moral or immoral. This reasoning method focuses on what morality is itself. Though not the focus of this book, Nietzsche's perspective that we choose our own values and should strive for a meaningful life above all else does have relevance to subsequent discussions in the book.

Justice

Western concepts of justice are derived from Greek tradition. The ancient maxim of justice is "to live honestly, to hurt no one, to give everyone his due." In ancient Greece, justice was believed to be derived from the order of society: a good society fostered justice, and justice fostered a good society.

Justice, in the Aristotelian tradition, means to treat equals equally, and to treat unequals unequally. A modern interpretation of the principle is sometimes expressed as follows: "Individuals should be treated the same, unless they are different in ways that are relevant to the situation in which they are involved."[41]

Justice is usually associated with issues of rights, fairness, and equality and, therefore, incorporates elements of both Kantian and utilitarian philosophy. A just act respects your rights and treats you fairly. Justice means giving each person what she or he deserves. *Justice* and *fairness* are closely related terms that are often used interchangeably, although differences do exist. Whereas justice usually is used to refer to a standard of rightness, fairness often is used to describe an ability to judge the effects of one's action without reference to one's feelings or interests.[42]

A useful example of justice is to say that if men and women do the same work, and there are no relevant differences between them or the work they are doing, then it is just to pay them the same wages.

Justice as a theory of action means to treat others fairly.

Treating others fairly means to treat them the same unless valid circumstances exist to do otherwise. Recall the earlier example in this chapter where a manager had to decide who would get a promotion: the more qualified employee or the well-liked one. Giving the promotion to the well-liked employee is unfair to the higher performer, who should be treated differently because there are valid reasons to do so in this case.

Justice is a personal virtue and is used in the discussions that follow as representative of the theory of justice.

Moral Nihilism and Friedrich Nietzsche

A brief examination of Nietzsche's theory is useful if for no other reason than to understand his objections to conventional morality. His views are not adopted in this book but do make one important point: people seek out meaning in life as the ultimate good. Meaning is sought not through conventional ethical values, according to Nietzsche, but, instead, through what he called "life-affirming values" that lead to individual development and human excellence, or human flourishing.

Nietzsche rejects the idea that moral judgments must be based on either the consequences of an act or the intentions of the acting person. He denies that we can ever know the intentions of any other human being. And because we have no knowledge of the future, neither can we know the consequences of an act. We may know the immediate consequences, but the facts may change and what at first appears as a good result may well in the long run turn out to have negative consequences.[43]

For example, what if we perceive wrongdoing in the workplace, so we report it up the chain of command. We decide to act based on how we interpreted the facts at the time, but it may turn out that the facts are different upon further investigation and the alleged wrongdoing was not wrong at all. So, our noble action may turn out to be a misreading of the situation.

Nietzsche did not think people sought happiness as an end in itself. Instead, he was dedicated to the idea that we are searching for meaning in life. Nietzsche's view of morality assigns great intrinsic value to the flourishing of "higher man." Higher types are solitary and deal with others only instrumentally—as a means to some other good for the solitary person. Thus, a human being who strives for something great considers everyone he meets along the way as a means to an end, an idea in direct opposition to Kantian ethics. A higher type seeks burdens and responsibilities in the pursuit of what is good for themselves.

Nietzsche challenges the idea of a morality as bound up with obligation, with codes and rules. He encourages individuals to think for themselves beyond conventional morality. His brand of ethics has been referred to as moral nihilism. *Nihilism* comes from the Latin *nihil*, or "nothing," which means "not anything," that which does not exist. By this view, ethical claims are generally false. A moral nihilist would say that nothing is morally good or bad, wrong or right because there are no moral truths. So, murder is not wrong, but neither is it right.

Nietzsche criticizes the concept of universality as objectionable because agents are relatively different, so a universal morality must necessarily be harmful to some. He believes that a culture in which moral norms prevail, such as Kantian respect for persons, utilitarianism, and altruistic behavior, will be a culture that eliminates the conditions for the realization of human excellence—the latter requiring concern with the self, struggle, and suffering. So happiness, according to Nietzsche, is not an intrinsically valuable end because suffering is positively necessary for the cultivation of individual development and a fulfilling life, which is the only thing that warrants admiration for Nietzsche.

Instead of the belief that there is a set of values or a course of action for all individuals, as assumed by conventional ethical reasoning, Nietzsche believes in each individual's sovereignty—the ability to make our own choices based on our own search for meaning. He believes that each of us needs to gain understanding, examine our perspectives, and reflect on our experiences. Skepticism, in the sense of questioning and challenging our existing beliefs and values, according to Nietzsche, is part of a radical reevaluation of our values and transformation of who we are, which is an ongoing process.

Perhaps the best way to sum up objections to Nietzsche's theory is that he seemed interested in promoting the development of human potential without regard for any specific morality or, even, any type of morality. His subjective and individualistic perspective was that each individual should seek meaning in life for reasons unrelated to any ethical theory.[44]

But, if each of us pursues our self-interest without regard to norms of behavior, then how can we ever go beyond improving our own well-being and improve the well-being of others?

The Language of Ethics

Understanding the terminology of ethics is essential to understanding how to behave ethically. The words *morals* and *ethics* are sometimes used interchangeably because they both deal with right and wrong behavior and the goodness or badness of human character. However, differences do exist. *Morals* refers to what a person, group, or society believes people should or should not do. Morals may be influenced by religious and cultural beliefs. For example, "Polygamy is always wrong" is the cultural belief, the moral, that the practice or custom of having more than one wife or husband at the same time is immoral. Describing something as moral typically means we believe it is good or right.

Ethics, on the other hand, is "the systematic and reasoned study of moral right and wrong, good and bad, including the principles and claims that employ these concepts."[45]

Ethics is based on well-founded (philosophical) standards of right and wrong that prescribe what individuals ought to do in specific situations, usually in terms of rights, obligations, benefits to society, fairness, or specific virtues.[46]

Ethical standards also relate to the norms of behavior for groups of professionals such as accountants, lawyers, and physicians.

Values are basic and fundamental beliefs that guide our actions. They are the intention behind purposeful action. Values refer to some standard or norm of behavior by which things can be evaluated. If we value honesty, then lying or deceiving others is wrongful behavior.

Whereas each of us can pick and choose which values we prioritize in life, as suggested by Nietzsche's life-affirming values, the purpose of this book is to explain ethical values that motivate ethical decision making. These values describe behavior that is right and good.

You might ask: What about my personal values? Is it wrong to seek out wealth, influence, and prestige—the values that drive my life? We can consider these ethically neutral values in themselves, but the morality of your personal values all depends on how you pursue these goals and use them. As suggested by enlightened egoism, there's nothing wrong with seeking wealth and a prominent position in life, so long as you don't use your status in a way that harms others. For example, using your wealth to fund charitable causes can benefit others while, at the same time, bringing greater meaning to your life.

In this sense, you see holding these values as an obligation to give back to society and contribute to the betterment of your community, as a civic duty. Exhibit 1.3 describes what three top philanthropists (Bill Gates, Mark Zuckerberg, and Michael Dell) gave to their charitable foundations in 2017.

Exhibit 1.3

The Ethics of Charitable Giving

The *Chronicle of Philanthropy* reported that for 2017, Microsoft cofounder Bill Gates and his wife, Melinda, gave Microsoft stock valued at about $4.6 billion to their $40 billion foundation, which supports global development, health, and policy, as well as efforts to improve the U.S. educational system. Priscilla Chan and Mark Zuckerberg were the second highest givers, contributing nearly $1.9 billion to their Chan Zuckerberg Foundation, which supports education, housing, science, and improving the criminal justice system. Dell Technologies founder Michael Dell and his wife, Susan, rounded out the top three with a $1 billion donation to their foundation, which supports programs in economic mobility, health, and urban education.[47]

There are different classifications of values in ethics. An *intrinsic value* is something that has value in its own right. It needs nothing outside itself to give it value; we value it for its own sake and not because it leads to something else. Suppose you were asked whether it is good to help others in their time of need. Most of us would say, yes, of course. Why? Because it's "good that people's needs be satisfied."[48]

We don't do it because it makes us feel better about ourselves, although that is quite likely.

An *extrinsic value* is something that has worth that is not intrinsic to it; it is valued because it leads to something else we value, or what philosophers call a derivative good. A job has extrinsic value because it enables us to receive money that goes toward our physiological needs—maintenance of the human body (food, water, warmth, rest). Without these needs met, we can't survive. The job may also bring us self-esteem and lend greater meaning to our life, but those are not its primary motivating factor; instead, they are outcomes that may be realized over time.

Generally, *principles* are rules governing behavior that are derived from values. There are different definitions of principles. The Josephson Institute of Ethics defines principles as "ethical values, translated into active language establishing standards or rules describing the kind of behavior an ethical person should and should not engage in."[49]

More to the point, *ethical principles* are "those general judgments that serve as a justification for particular ethical prescriptions and evaluations of human actions."[50]

The appeal of this definition is that it applies to our actions, which is the last step in the four-component decision-making process described in Figure 1.1. These principles enable us to analyze alternatives and choose a course of action using the ethical reasoning methods discussed in the previous section.

Now that you are familiar with the language of ethics, the next step is to apply it to ethical behavior.

Ethical Decision Making

James Rest (1941–1999), an American psychologist who specialized in moral psychology and development, identified a four-component model of ethical behavior that we can use in the decision-making process. His model explains what needs to be in place for us to take ethical action: ethical awareness, ethical judgment, and ethical intention that lead to ethical action. Figure 1.1 depicts the four concepts and how they relate to the seven-step ethical decision-making framework named in the Introduction. So, the framework described in the Introduction is being modified as shown in Figure 1.1 to accommodate Rest's model. This is the process that we will use to analyze ethical issues in Chapters 4 and 5.

Ethical behavior starts with ethical awareness. *Ethical awareness* is "the ability of an individual to recognize an ethical issue, problem, or dilemma."[51]

It begins with an understanding that our actions affect the welfare of others and a willingness to examine the implications of our own behavior on the lives of others.

Once we have identified the ethical issues, the next step is to make *ethical judgments* about what "ideally" ought to be done to resolve the ethical dilemma. This process of ethical judgment requires that we identify and analyze the ethics of the alternatives. Ethical judgments depend on our ability to reason through ethical dilemmas and determine the best course of action. This type of ethical reasoning was previously discussed and is summarized in Table 1.2.

To effectively reason through ethical issues and make ethical judgments, you must have *ethical intent*, which means you are motivated to do the right thing and will decide on a course of action on the basis of your intentions. Our motivation to act ethically depends on our willingness to prioritize ethical values (e.g., honesty, trust, kindness, and compassion) over non-ethical ones, such as power, prestige, and fortune.

With ethical awareness, ethical judgment, and ethical intention, the final step in Rest's four-component model is *ethical action*. Once we've decided what to do and are committed to doing it, we need to summon the courage to act ethically even in the face of countervailing forces. First, we should check ourselves and ask whether we would be satisfied with our intended action and whether it is defensible. Then, we should behave ethically. Our intention to act ethically may not be aligned with ethical action if we lack *ethical character*. Having an ethical character, as previously discussed, means possessing ethical values or virtues that are directed to rightful behavior.

Figure 1.1
Ethical Decision-Making Process

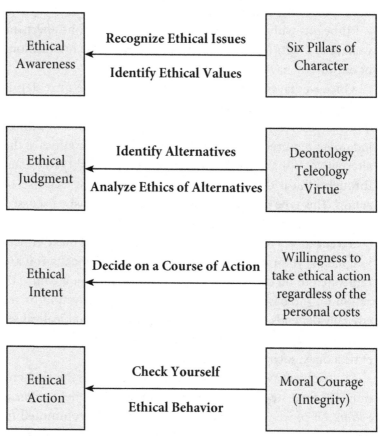

The best way to learn about ethical behavior is to apply the ethical theories in an actual or imagined situation. We will apply the theories using the process in Figure 1.1 to the ghosting example and then to assumed and real-world examples in Chapters 4 and 5.

Ghosting in a Dating Relationship

Ghosting occurs when someone you believe cares about you, such as a person you have been dating, disappears from contact without any explanation—no phone call, email, or text.[52] According to the online relationship and dating blog Plenty of Fish, in a survey of eight hundred millennial daters between the ages of eighteen and thirty-three, almost 80 percent of singles have been ghosted. Many of those ghosted have likely done it to someone else.[53]

Sally has dated Bill twice. She doesn't share his desire to maintain a relationship. Should she contact Bill and explain?

The Golden Rule is always a good place to start. Sally should ask: What would she want Bill to do or say if their roles were reversed and he wished to discontinue relations with her? Sally might think that she wouldn't care if Bill suddenly stopped responding to her because no response can be assumed to be indifference, so she'd just forget about him after one or two attempts at contact. On the other hand, Sally might reason that, if she were in Bill's shoes, knowing for sure why the relationship has ended would put her mind at ease.

So, in ethical reasoning, it's important to know which values are important to you. Kindness and empathy would dictate she tell Bill and explain why she broke off the relationship. A different person, on the other hand, for whom kindness and empathy were not such high priorities, might decide what to do solely based on self-interest, which might mean continuing to ghost Bill because that enables Sally to maintain her equilibrium by not having to confront him on the dating issue.

Decision-Making Process

The following analysis is based on the decision-making process depicted in Figure 1.1.

> *Ethical awareness:* The ethical issue for Sally is whether to tell Bill about her true feelings. The ethical values of the Six Pillars of Character at issue here are trustworthiness, respect, caring, and responsibility.

> *Ethical judgment:* Here, Sally could use deontology, teleology, and virtue ethics to analyze the ethical issues, identify the alternative courses of action, and apply ethical reasoning to decide what to do.

> *Ethical intent:* What motivates Sally to act? What is her reason for informing Bill or not? Ethical action won't take place unless Sally's decision is based on rightful intent. Sally should be willing to act ethically regardless of the personal costs.

> *Ethical action:* A person of integrity has the moral courage to carry through an ethical decision with ethical action. Before doing so, Sally should check herself to be certain that her intended decision is the most ethical one by asking: How would she feel if her decision was made public by Bill and, for example, was discussed on social media? Would she be able to defend it? Considering whether we would stand by our decision in the face of public scrutiny is a quick way to test whether

we're doing the right thing even if we do not get called out.

Virtue Ethics

Recall that virtue is the notion that certain attributes (i.e., ethical values) become excellences of character with practice. Sally might use the following reasoning to analyze the ethical issues at stake in the situation and see how they would be resolved if she were to behave according to specific virtues.

Caring: Sally should place herself in Bill's position. A caring, empathetic person can relate to another's feelings and consider them in deciding what to do.

Trustworthiness: Sally would be committing a lie by omission if she fails to tell Bill about her true feelings. This is not an act of a trustworthy person.

Responsibility: Sally is accountable for her actions. She's decided not to date Bill anymore, so she should accept personal responsibility for her decision. Summoning up the courage to inform Bill builds character.

According to virtue ethics, Sally should inform Bill why she doesn't want to pursue the relationship so he's not left wondering. She may not feel comfortable addressing the issue with Bill or be happy about having to do it, but Sally should feel pride that she's doing the right thing. This kind of action can increase self-respect, enhance her self-esteem, and build her virtuous character. Owning up to one's decisions takes moral courage.

Ethical Egoism

Sally seeks to promote her own good, so she would decide not to inform Bill about her decision.

Enlightened Egoism

Here, Sally considers how her actions might affect Bill. What value does she place on informing Bill? It's hard to know what she would do without understanding her feelings. Still, we could reason that as long as informing Bill does not hinder her ability to satisfy her own interests, Sally should inform Bill.

Utilitarianism

The choices for Sally are simple: inform Bill about her feelings or don't. Here are possible reasons for Sally *not* to tell Bill:

- She doesn't want to cause Bill pain or hurt his feelings.
- It's too emotional for her to address her feelings.
- Not communicating with him sends the message there is no relationship going forward.

Notice how these are rationalizations for not dealing with Bill. They're not based on any moral reason, such as treating Bill with compassion.

Sally might want to tell Bill for the following reasons:

- She won't have to deal with further phone calls and texts from Bill.
- Communicating about her decision could relieve Bill's anxiety about why she disappeared. Bill may fear the unknown: Was she injured or worse?

- Feedback enables Bill to reflect on his behavior and make needed changes for future relationships if necessary. Was it something he said or did?
- It provides closure for both Sally and Bill.

Notice how these reasons focus on how Sally's actions might affect Bill, on the consequences of her action. They're not solely based on her self-interest.

Sally may not feel happy about informing Bill, but it should provide a measure of satisfaction in that she acted thoughtfully. Sally should consider as a check on the process how she would feel if Bill takes to the internet and criticizes her silence. Maybe her friends and even future dating partners see his posts. They may be critical of how Sally handled the matter. Is this the way she wants to be known on the dating circuit?

Consequentialism has its challenges because it's sometimes difficult to know with certainty whether the consequences of our actions will be good or bad. What if Bill is more enraged when Sally contacts him? He tells her she was thoughtless, caused him pain, and is not a good person. Maybe Sally shouldn't have said anything.

Another problem is consequentialism might lead to rationalizing otherwise unethical actions by claiming the good outweighs the bad even though the bad is substantial. Sally might reason that it's more important or beneficial for her to avoid a conflict with Bill and hope he simply forgets about it over time, even though she knows he's been agonizing over not knowing why she stopped all communication.

These are act utilitarian considerations. Looking at rule utilitarianism, we might say that Sally shouldn't take an action that violates the rule "never lie to another person." Failing to inform Bill is untruthful because she omits information that is surely important to him. It's a lie by omission.

Deontology

Does Sally have a moral duty to inform Bill of why she decided to no longer pursue a relationship? Given that Bill should be treated with dignity and Sally has an obligation to respect him as a human being, it would seem that Sally does have a moral duty to discuss the matter with Bill, assuming she is a person of good will. Moreover, we can assume she would want Bill to discuss the matter with her if their roles were reversed, because doing so is a universal act and not conditioned by one's own self-interest. It is right to discuss such a matter with your dating partner in each and every situation.

If we assume Sally has a moral duty to inform Bill, then by virtue of her strength of good will she should discuss the matter even if it doesn't bring her happiness. Nevertheless, fulfilling her moral duty can add meaning to her life.

What Should Sally Do?

Like most ethical decisions, the best choice of action will depend on Sally's motivations and intentions. If she seeks to promote her own interest, Bill probably won't be told unless Sally views it in her best interest to tell him, perhaps because it brings closure to the issue. If she looks at the situation from Bill's perspective, then she's likely to inform him because doing so treats him as an end in himself and not a means for Sally to satisfy her self-interest. It's also the caring and empathetic way to deal with the situation.

In making ethical decisions, it's sometimes useful to look at things from a different perspective. Sally might consider how she would feel if she interviewed for a job at a firm that did not communicate its hiring decision and left her hanging about whether she got the job or didn't. If her attempts to find out are to no avail, she might wonder: Did I get the job? Should I interview further? Presumably, Sally would feel she has a right to know whether she got the job and how she did on the interview. Thinking about her situation with Bill, she might then understand why it is important to communicate her feelings to him and not leave him hanging.

Conclusion

It has been said that we can make ethics part of our daily lives by asking each day: How am I doing at the art of ethical behavior? How many times have you asked yourself: Is that the way I should treat someone else? Is that the way someone else should treat me? We have the ability to critically analyze our interpersonal behavior, develop standards of right and wrong and good and bad, and apply those standards in everyday situations. These moral standards, plus a set of virtuous character traits, are what we strive for when we talk about acting ethically.[54]

We can transform our life through ethical behavior and gain happiness and greater meaning. We do this by valuing others as human beings, considering their interests as well as our own, thinking about how our intended actions might affect others, reflecting on our moral duties to others, and seeking out ways to lead a more fulfilling life.

Ethical behavior has specific purposes: to enhance the well-being of ourselves and others. In the next chapter you will learn how to practice ethical behavior and avoid the obstacles that prevent it from occurring.

CHAPTER 2

Practicing Ethical Behavior

Action indeed is the sole medium of expression for ethics.

—Jane Addams

Jane Addams, known as the mother of social work, was a public philosopher, author, leader in women's suffrage, and advocate for world peace. She makes the point that ethical behavior depends on our actions. Recall from Chapter 1, our actions say a lot about the kind of person we are and what motivates us to act. Knowing how to act ethically provides the tools and perspective to do so when ethical dilemmas arise.

Have you heard the proverb "Practice makes perfect"? It means doing something again and again is the best way to learn it. You develop the skills to complete a task or meet your obligations to others. It seems logical that if you do something frequently, you will get better and better at it. Ethics is no different.

We practice ethics through the choices we make, knowing

the reasons for our choices, and the actions we take to carry through ethical intent with ethical actions. We develop an *ethical sense.*

Ethics is a contact sport. Practicing ethics occurs best in our relationships with others. Knowing what promotes ethical behavior and what might make it more difficult to achieve establishes the signposts that lead us to embrace the helpful attributes while steering clear of the roadblocks. You can learn how to make a safe journey on the road to happiness and meaning by applying the principles of ethical behavior in your personal relationships, workplace interactions, and social networking activities, and by repeating these behaviors at every turn.

The Markkula Center for Applied Ethics at Santa Clara University suggests you ask yourself five questions to set the stage for discovering whether you have practiced being ethical today, which can be explained as follows.[55]

Did I practice virtues today? Was I honest today? Kind to others? Did I show compassion and empathy?

Did I do more good than harm today? Did my actions benefit others while avoiding harm to them?

Did I treat people with dignity and respect today? Did I hold others in high regard?

Was I fair and just today? Did I treat others rightly?

Was my community better because I was in it? Was I better because I was in my community? Did I act in a way that improves the quality of life for me and others?

Elizabeth McGrath, a psychologist who writes about cultural ethical beliefs, points out that the largest contribution an individual can make to uplifting the ethical climate in society is to act in the most ethical way, thereby modeling for society another way to live rather than by pursuing one's selfish interests. "People need to see good ethics in action before they will believe that it is truly possible."[56]

McGrath asks the question: "How can we begin to create behaviors that encourage and nourish the goodness in others instead of killing it?" She suggests it occurs "slowly, deliberately, and with great effort. It starts by becoming more conscious of the importance of such behaviors and let[ting] go of destructive habits and ways of thinking that discourage ethical behaviors."[57]

There are a variety of ways to practice being ethical in everyday life. We can develop good habits, practice kindness, be courageous, act in the best interests of others, build moral muscle memory, concentrate on the means, not the ends, and create a more civil society. What follows is a discussion of these and other ways to act that promote ethical behavior and avoid behaviors that prevent it from happening. Before addressing these behaviors, it's important to understand how being ethical relates to following the law.

Law Abiding

Laws are rules and regulations that come with penalties and punishments if they are not followed. Ethical behaviors, on the other hand, are societal norms that are based on moral principles and values. Ethics is what should be done—it is good conduct—whereas laws deal with behavior that is compelled. Ethics can be legislated by laying out a system of duties, as do laws against killing, stealing, kidnapping, and others that are based on ethical standards. But not all ethical behaviors are laws.

Generally, people equate following the law with being ethical.

There is no doubt this is true. However, it is also important to understand that laws set minimum standards of ethical behavior. They don't address every situation. Ethical people analyze the requirements of law of each situation and decide what to do based on the laws and other ethical principles, such as the categorical imperative.

In some cases, following the law leads to greater harm than breaking it. For example, the law may not prohibit an act that would be widely condemned as unethical. Before the Civil War in the United States, slaves and indentured servants were considered personal property in a legal institution of chattel enslavement. Though slavery was legal, few looking back would say keeping slaves was an ethical practice.

On a more basic level, betraying someone's trust may not be illegal, but most people would consider it unethical. The contrary is true as well: the law also can prohibit acts that some groups would perceive as ethical. For instance, speeding is illegal, but many people do not perceive an ethical conflict with exceeding the speed limit while driving.

Benjamin Disraeli (1804–1881) was a noted English novelist, debater, and the United Kingdom's former prime minister. He said, "When men are pure, laws are useless; when men are corrupt, laws are broken."

What Disraeli meant is a person of good will honors and respects the rules and laws and is willing to go beyond them when circumstances warrant, and yet, ethical people do not need rules and laws to guide their actions. They always try to do the right thing. On the other hand, the existence of specific laws prohibiting certain behaviors will not stop a person who is unethical (e.g., does not care about others) from violating those laws.[58] Instances of sexual harassment of Hollywood stars that were disclosed in 2016 and that grew the #MeToo movement are examples of such unethical behavior.

Developing Good Habits

The 7 Habits of Highly Effective People, written by Stephen R. Covey, is one of the best-selling books on self-improvement of all time and one of the most influential. A brief summary about Covey and his basic philosophy appears in Exhibit 2.1.

Exhibit 2.1

Stephen R. Covey

Stephen R. Covey (1932–2012) is known for his classic book, *The 7 Habits of Highly Effective People*. His self-improvement book has sold more than twenty-five million copies worldwide since its first publication in 1989 and has been translated into thirty-eight languages. In 1996, *Time* magazine named Covey one of the twenty-five most influential people.

The 7 Habits presents an inside-out approach to human effectiveness that is centered on principles and character. *Inside-out* means that change starts within oneself. Covey contends that many people who have achieved a high degree of outward success still find themselves struggling with the inner need to develop personal effectiveness and develop healthy relationships with other people.

Though the success literature of the last half of the twentieth century largely attributed success to a philosophy of the personality ethic—personality traits, skills, techniques, and maintaining a positive attitude—Covey maintains that we need to return to the character ethic that preceded it, which emphasizes deeper principles to guide long-term relationships.[59]

In the book, Covey refers to a *character ethic*, meaning a way of behaving in which you align your values with "universal and timeless" principles such as fairness, integrity, honesty, truthfulness, and respect. His seven principles are deep, fundamental truths that are universal: they apply in any situation, in any culture, and are found in the world's major religions.[60] Thus, they include components of the ethical values that form the basis of the Golden Rule.

The seven habits include: (1) be proactive; (2) begin with the end in mind; (3) put first things first; (4) think win-win; (5) seek first to understand, then to be understood; (6) synergize; and (7) sharpen the saw. The habits discussed below are those that deal most directly with ethical behavior.

Covey contends in the first habit—be proactive—that what distinguishes us as humans from all other animals is our inherent ability to examine our own character, to decide how to view ourselves and our situations, and to control our own effectiveness.[61] This is important because it implies we can learn the art of ethical behavior and apply it to life's circumstances.

In his second habit—begin with the end in mind—he raises the question: What are we trying to accomplish? This is similar to asking: How can we be happy with life's circumstances? What is the end goal of life? How can we achieve greater meaning through our actions?

In his fifth habit—seek first to understand, then to be understood—Covey points out that most people listen with the intent to reply, not to understand. We listen to ourselves as we prepare in our mind what we are going to say and the questions we are going to ask. We filter everything we hear through our life experiences, our frame of reference. And consequently, we decide prematurely what the other person means before he or she finishes communicating. Covey refers to *empathetic listening* as an important skill. With this type of listening, you listen until the other person feels understood. Empathetic listeners listen for meaning. They listen for behavior.[62] Empathetic people are open to others' ideas and feelings. They don't lash out whenever they disagree. Empathetic people show they care by their actions. They seek to connect emotionally.

Robin Sharma, a respected expert in leadership and personal mastery, suggests that each of us take just one day to make the decision to listen masterfully. "Don't interrupt. Don't rehearse your answer while the other person is speaking. And don't dare check your email or search for text messages while another human being is sharing their words. Just listen. Just hear. Just be there for that person."[63]

Practicing Kindness

Kind acts come in many forms. Practicing kindness toward others shows we value those individuals and are willing to go out of our way to help them. Helping others helps us because it enhances our feelings of self-worth. You can practice good deeds for others that you plan ahead, such as the following:

- Cook a meal for a friend or neighbor who is recovering at home after surgery.

- Feed and walk your neighbors' dogs while they are out of town so the dogs do not have to go to a kennel.

- Volunteer at a food bank or organize a charitable event in your community.

- Write a thank-you note (not an email) to someone who did something nice for you.

You may have heard the expression to *practice random acts of kindness*. Random kind acts are unplanned; they are spontaneous. You may do them because of the way you feel at the moment. Have you ever done any of the following?

- Help an elderly or infirm person cross the street.

- Watch the young child of a neighbor while he or she goes to the store.

- Invite a new employee on their first day at work to join you for lunch.

- Offer to cover the shift of a coworker who has a family emergency.

These may seem like small things, but kindness to one person can lead to their being kind to another. One form of kindness is to pay it forward. *To pay it forward* means to respond to a kindness you have received by being kind to someone else. Rather than paying it back to the person who did something nice for you, you pay it forward to a different person and hope others do the same.

A great example of paying it forward occurred spontaneously one morning in August 2014, when a customer at a drive-through Starbucks in St. Petersburg, Florida, paid for her own iced coffee and then paid for the caramel macchiato of the driver behind her, who then did the same, paying for the drink of the next customer in line. People ordered a drink at the speaker, and when they pulled through to the next window, the barista said with a smile that their beverage had already been paid for by the person in front of them. According to the *Tampa Bay Times*, by six in the evening 378 customers ordering drinks had also paid for the order of the stranger behind them.[64]

Practicing random acts of kindness and paying it forward show we care about others. Knowing you have done something nice for another can bring happiness and enhance your well-being. It's a selfless act; we expect nothing in return other than hoping the person we have helped will do good things for others. It's a thoughtful act that can give us a warm feeling. Imagine if everyone in a community acted in this manner. It would advance civility in a tangible way.

Acting with Moral Courage

One definition of *moral courage* is doing the right thing even at the risk of inconvenience, ridicule, punishment, or loss of job, security, or social status.[65] Moral courage means to act for moral reasons despite the risk of adverse consequences. Courage is a moral virtue when our actions are motivated by good intentions. Aristotle viewed courage as the mean, or average, on a continuum of levels of confidence in the face of fearful situations. It lies between the opposing extremes of cowardice, on the one hand, and rashness, on the other.[66]

A good example of when it would have been important to act with moral courage is the hazing incident that occurred at Louisiana State University in the 2018 fall semester. Members of Delta Kappa Epsilon forced pledges to lie in piles of broken glass, kicked them with steel-toed boots, urinated on them, and committed other acts of abuse. Additional details about the incident appear in Exhibit 2.2.

Exhibit 2.2

Hazing Incident at LSU

In addition to the hazing actions described, some pledges had gasoline poured on them naked, were forced to submerge themselves in icy water, were burned with cigarettes, and were beaten with a metal pipe. The fraternity's national organization closed the LSU chapter. The university charged the abusers with felony second-degree battery and false imprisonment. Nine fraternity members were arrested by the police on February 16, 2019. One student was charged with the most serious crime of the group: three felonies for battery and false imprisonment and three charges of criminal hazing.

Imagine you are a fraternity brother witnessing these incidents. Recognizing the dangers to the pledges, you want to do something about it but are concerned about the reaction of your fraternity brothers. If you jump in at that moment, you, too, may be forced to endure abuse, either verbal or physical.

If you do nothing, then you allow your fear of the consequences to get in the way of doing the right thing. If you act with moral courage, you would do something about the situation while also minimizing the risk of harm to yourself. So, what can you do? Speaking to the brothers and discussing the dangers is a start. Much like whistleblowing, the first attempt should be to take care of the matter internally among the people directly involved. If that doesn't work, reporting the matter to the authorities, in this case the Interfraternity Council that works with the university administration, should be the next step.

Never assume someone else will do what you are in a unique position to do. The hazing incident illustrates the phenomenon of the *bystander effect*, where those who can change the outcome of an event stand back and do nothing, hoping or rationalizing that others will step forward. Letting the hazing go on without speaking out implies tacit approval of the practice and is not acting with moral courage.

Acting in the Interests of Others

Egoism is a strong motivating factor for action. People generally act out of what they think to be in their best interest (it will achieve their needs and wants). We can act out of self-interest and still be ethical when our motivation is to do good things for others. Doing good deeds for others, such as a random act of kindness, can bring us happiness. It can also make us feel good about ourselves—build self-esteem—as when we report the illegal dumping of toxic waste to stop the practice of poisoning the drinking water of local residents. It also takes moral courage to do so. Linda Fisher Thornton, the CEO of the leadership development firm Leading in Context and adjunct associate professor of ethics and leadership at the University of Richmond, raises the question: Can we be ethical without considering others and acting in ways that benefit them? The following questions about ethics and self-interest are identified in her piece "'Ethics' Means Acting Beyond Self-Interest."[67]

1. *Is ethics moving beyond the ego to show concern for others?* Ethics traditionally assumes that human beings are also capable of acting from a concern for others that is not derived from a quest for their own well-being.

2. *Can we define ethics based on reason, when reason doesn't involve others?* Our reason for acting must go beyond our own well-being if we are to develop truly meaningful relationships and better the lives of ourselves and others.

3. *If we serve others now, will we benefit long term?* Enlightened egoism in ethics states that persons who act to further the interests of others ultimately serve their self-interest. Pursuing enlightened egoism means that we may need to sacrifice short-term benefits to ourselves to maximize the long-term interests for ourselves and others.

According to the philosopher Immanuel Kant, for an act to have moral worth it must be undertaken out of a sense of duty. When we act solely out of self-interest, we preclude the possibility of our action being a moral one.[68] We're not thinking of others and what our moral obligation to them is as a member of humanity. So, acting out of self-interest must have a moral purpose. In the hazing incident, you have a moral duty to stop pain and suffering.

Building Moral Muscle Memory

Being ethical requires consistent behavior. We shouldn't pick and choose when to be ethical. We can liken being an ethical person to building a skill. If you want to be a consummate weightlifter, practice lifting weights whenever you can. If you want to be ethical, practice building *moral muscle memory* by making ethical choices whenever you can.

Our moral muscle memory kicks in when we are in a heightened physiological or psychological state as a result of an ethical challenge, so our body will react automatically and we can anticipate and rehearse the kind of responses that may be effective to counteract the reasons and rationalizations others give for questionable behavior.

According to Mary Gentile, the developer of "Giving Voice to Values," a technique used to help people act on their values, we can build moral muscle memory by anticipating and rehearsing the kinds of responses to ethical challenges that may be effective in countering the objections we may hear from others so that our minds react automatically even if we are frozen intellectually. Our mind will default to our moral voice, enabling us to speak up and act on our values.[69] Think about how you might use your moral muscle memory when we examine everyday ethics situations later.

Focusing on the Means to an End, Not the End Itself

One of the more common questions in ethics is: Does the "end justify the means?" In other words, does a good outcome excuse any questionable behaviors or acts along the way there? Indeed, the essence of utilitarianism holds that the end does justify the means if the means chosen bring the greatest benefit and minimize the most harm to stakeholders (i.e., ourselves as the decision maker and others affected by our intended action).

The answer to this question depends on what the ends or goals are and what means are used to achieve them. If the goals are good and honorable and the means used to achieve them are also good and honorable, then it is generally considered that the ends do justify the means.[70] Stopping dangerous hazing practices protects the health and welfare of the pledges, and reporting the hazing first to the fraternity and, if necessary, to the Interfraternity Council is the right way to go about it.

Questions about whether the end goal justifies the means used to achieve it arises in everyday ethics. Those who emphasize the ends over the means undervalue the means used to accomplish one's goals. In a sense this results from a lack of ethical awareness. Here are a few examples.

- Cheating on exams in college (the means) is okay if you will graduate with honors and get a good job (the end)

- Lying on a résumé to qualify for a job without possessing the necessary credentials (the means) is justified if it allows you to get the job (the end)

- Posting sexually provocative photos of someone you dated after he or she broke up with you (the means) is alright if it provides relief from your suffering (the end)

What's wrong, specifically, with the actions above? Cheating on exams to get a better job puts other students at a competitive disadvantage (unjust behavior). Lying on a résumé misleads the potential employer about your abilities and could lead to an unjustified hiring (dishonest; lack of personal responsibility). Posting provocative photos to get even means using someone else in a harmful manner to accomplish your goals (uncaring; lack of empathy). In each case, the actions taken are motivated by self-interest without regard to how they affect others.

If, as this book contends, our end goals in life are to achieve happiness and greater meaning, then we should treat others in a way that promotes our well-being and theirs. The way we treat others—the things we say or do—is the means to promote happiness and meaning through ethical behavior. We can't truly have a civil society if we dismiss the needs of others and focus solely on what we want out of life.

Creating a More Civil Society

By age sixteen, George Washington had copied out by hand *110 Rules of Civility & Decent Behavior in Company and Conversation*. These rules are based on a set of guidelines composed by French Jesuits in 1595. The first rule is: "Every Action done in Company, ought to be with Some Sign of

Respect, to those that are Present."[71] The fact that Washington recognized respect many years ago emphasizes its place as an enduring moral value in society and important component of civility.

Civility is about more than just politeness. It is about disagreeing without disrespecting, seeking common ground as a starting point for dialogue about differences, listening past one's preconceptions, and teaching others to do the same.[72] Indeed, "civility represents a long tradition of moral virtues essential to democracy. Virtues like empathy, humility, integrity, honesty, and respect for others are ideals of democratic engagement."[73]

Tomas Spath and Cassandra Dahnke, writing for the Institute for Civility in Government, characterize civility as "claiming and caring for one's identity, needs, and beliefs without degrading someone else's in the process."[74] This is a useful characterization because it links actions that benefit ourselves with treating others respectfully.

Writing for *Psychology Today* online, Thomas Plante, a clinical psychiatrist and behavioral scientist, provides helpful ideas on how to be more civil:[75]

- Think before speaking.
- Focus on facts rather than beliefs and opinions.
- Focus on common good rather than individual agendas.
- Disagree with others respectfully.
- Maintain an openness to others without hostility.
- Be respectful of diverse views and groups.
- Embody a spirit of collegiality.

- Offer productive and corrective feedback to those who behave in demeaning, insulting, disrespectful, and discriminatory ways.

An annual poll on civility in society by Weber Shandwick continues to show that a vast majority of Americans—93 percent—identify a civility problem in society, with most classifying it as a "major" problem (69%). Eight in ten Americans (84%) have at one time or another experienced incivility in a wide variety of circumstances, most typically while shopping (39%), while driving (39%), or while on social media (38%).[76]

It seems today, more than ever before, we are witnessing uncivil behavior in broad swathes of society. We hear about one group of people with a distinct point of view making offensive comments to others with an opposing view. Some get in the face of a politician they don't like to forcefully put their point across and do the same in private venues. Arguments break out that more frequently lead to violence, so the police are called in to maintain order. On college campuses, we increasingly hear about some students shouting down or walking out on speakers because they don't like the speaker's message. What's lost is the ability to have a productive dialogue about our differences. In a 2017 Gallup survey on civility on college campuses, 61 percent of students, up from 54 percent in 2016, say campus climate prevents people from speaking freely because others might be offended.[77]

Incivility occurs because we lose sight of what it means to be an ethical person. Ethical people do not berate others. They certainly don't promote violent behavior. Being willing to accept the ideas of others who may not agree with you is a sign of civil behavior. It values those with opposing views as members of humanity. To bring civility back to society, we all need to learn how to discuss contentious issues without being insulting. Trolling is a good example of incivility. Trolling on the internet occurs when a person starts quarrels or upsets people by posting inflammatory or off-topic messages. Trolls purposefully say controversial things to provoke others. Trolls hide behind their electronic devices, screen names, and avatars when they go out trolling for trouble, and after they are all done, the target of their behavior is left to pick up the pieces. Trolls seem to be on the prowl for their next victim, ready to pounce and offend others through inappropriate comment posts, harassment, and other discriminatory behaviors.

If you have been the victim of trolling, as have I, you wonder when the troll will strike next and what effect it might have on your happiness—at least for that day. Germany Kent, a social media etiquette expert, said about behavior online: "Tweet others the way you want to be tweeted."

Michael Brannigan, the Plaff Endowed Chair in Ethics and Moral Values at the College of St. Rose in Albany, New York, observed, "Civility cultivates a civic code of decency. It requires us to discipline our impulses for the sake of others. It demands we free ourselves from self-absorption. Civility is that moral glue without which our society could come apart."[78] Given the scope of incivility in our daily lives, each of us should look for ways to control these negative behaviors that can cause unhappiness for ourselves and others. One way to build a better, more civil society is to advance the cause of greater ethics.

What Makes It More Difficult to Act Ethically?

Selfish Behavior versus Self-ish

There is a difference between acting in our self-interest and selfishness. Merriam-Webster defines *selfish* as being concerned excessively or exclusively with oneself: seeking or concentrating on one's own pleasure or well-being without regard for others. Personal success coach Krissy Jackson points out that selfishness in the negative sense, as this definition implies, is not good behavior because it's about living your life at the expense of others. Instead, she focuses on being *self-ish:* "about being loving, kind and caring towards yourself; . . . honoring the commitments you make to yourself; . . . taking care of you in all aspects—body, mind, and spirit. Without this attitude of self-care and nurturing, you are no use to anyone—not to yourself and certainly not to others."[79]

This is an interesting perspective because we do need to attend to our own needs to be able to serve others. If we are chronically sick, emotionally disturbed, or ethically challenged, then it's unlikely we can improve the lives of others and, as a result, gain happiness and greater meaning in life. We might think of being self-ish as a prerequisite to happiness. It also fits in with the discussion in the next chapter of a hierarchy of needs that leads to self-actualization.

Ethical Relativism

Ethical relativism is a theory that holds there are no universal, permanent criteria to determine what may or may not be an ethical action. Thus, what's right or wrong and good or bad is not absolute but variable and relative, depending on the person, circumstances, and social situation. For the ethical relativist, there are no universal moral standards—standards that can be universally applied to all peoples at all times. The only moral standards against which a society's practices can be judged are its own. If ethical relativism is correct, then there can be no common framework for resolving moral disputes or for reaching agreement on ethical matters among members of different societies. Nietzsche's moral nihilism takes this kind of approach in addressing what is and is not ethical.

A good example of ethical relativism is apartheid in South Africa. Starting in 1948, the ruling party began enforcing existing policies of racial segregation under a system where nonwhite South Africans, who were in the majority, were forced to live in separate areas from white people and use separate facilities, not unlike the segregation in the United States. Despite strong and consistent opposition to apartheid, it was in effect for the better part of fifty years, only finally starting to be repealed in 1991.

The majority of white people may have believed it was an ethically appropriate practice to institutionalize racial discrimination, and legislative decisions were made on that basis, but surely apartheid can't be called an ethical practice. Who would want to be treated as a second-class citizen? If everyone discriminated against everyone else, society would likely fall into chaos and governing would become virtually impossible. What's the answer? At a minimum, there needs to be a universally accepted standard of behavior, such as the Golden Rule.

One form of ethical relativism is situational ethics. A *situational ethic* is consequence-based as well as relativistic. So, no actions are intrinsically correct/wrong, and no actions are absolutely correct/right. Much like ethical relativism, situational ethics is contextual.

Situational ethics was pioneered by Joseph Fletcher. In situational ethics, right and wrong depend on the facts of each situation rather than prescribed norms of behavior such as the Golden Rule. There are no universal moral rules or rights—each case is unique and deserves a unique solution. Ethical decisions should follow flexible guidelines rather than absolute rules and be taken on a case-by-case basis. Because circumstances alter cases, a situationist would hold that in practice what at some times and places might be called right in other times and places we might call wrong.[80]

The problem with situational ethics, much like with ethical relativism, is we leave it up to each individual and the circumstances encountered to determine right from wrong. There is no common denominator norm of behavior. So, one fraternity brother might believe hazing is an acceptable practice regardless of any harms to a pledge because it is a rite of passage. Another might say it's wrong regardless of the purpose because it can harm others. Yet a third might say it's acceptable in some cases when the hazing is in good fun and harms no one but unacceptable when it goes too far and harms a pledge. With such an approach to decision making, choosing what to do can be relegated to a debate between those with different points of view rather than an evaluation based on an accepted standard of behavior, such as the universality perspective in Kantian ethics (see Chapter 1).

Applying a situational ethic can lead to rationalizing unethical actions. For example, assume a coworker steals money from the company and you find out about it. You approach your coworker to tell him it's wrong, and he then admits doing the act. Consider the following situations:

1. The coworker gave no good reason to steal the money other than greed and self-interest. Do you tell the boss about the theft?

2. The coworker promised to pay back the money immediately and asked you not to report him. Do you tell the boss about the theft?

3. The coworker shares with you that his wife is under-
   going expensive cancer treatment and they don't have
   enough money to pay for it. The coworker tells you
   he expects to get a loan from a family member with
   which he will pay back the company. Do you tell the
   boss about the theft?

In each case, the circumstances are different, but the decision
should not be. Stealing is wrong and we'd have an ethical
obligation to tell the boss. We may feel deeply sorry about our
coworker's wife's cancer. Still, letting our personal feelings get
in the way of doing the right thing because, we rationalize,
the situation allows for it makes it difficult to practice ethical
behavior consistently. It also involves us in a cover-up
that may make it more difficult if a similar situation arises in
the future.

Incivility

The thoughtlessness of some behaviors and comments can
cause distress, thereby affecting the well-being of others and,
in turn, our own happiness. Here are a few behaviors that are
uncivil:

- Making the discussion all about yourself—all the
  time—thereby frustrating others.

- Making infuriating comments designed to provoke
  another to respond.

- Demeaning others and attacking their character.

- Getting the last word in so you prevent the other
  person from making a good point at the end of the
  discussion.

Many of these behaviors are passive-aggressive, meaning they are negative behaviors that are expressed in an unassertive but harming way. The best way to deal with them and avoid further uncivil acts is not to overreact, get drawn into the game, or try to change the other's thoughts or behaviors. In addition to the acts of incivility discussed above that can create disharmony, incivility in the workplace can disrupt the ethical culture of an organization. Writing for the *Harvard Business Review* online, professors Christine Porath and Christine Pearson define *workplace incivility* as the exchange of seemingly inconsequential and inconsiderate words and deeds that violate conventional norms of workplace conduct.[81]

According to Diane Berenbaum, who writes on human resource issues for the HR Exchange Network, incivility in the workplace can take the following forms:[82]

- Rude or obnoxious behavior
- Badgering or back-stabbing
- Withholding important customer/client information
- Sabotaging a project or damaging someone's reputation

Others that may be less invasive include the following:

- Arriving late to a meeting
- Checking email or texting during a meeting
- Not answering calls or responding to emails in a timely manner
- Ignoring or interrupting a colleague
- Not saying "please" or thank you"

Berenbaum notes the consequences of incivility in the workplace on employee behavior:[83]

- Being less engaged, which can lead to being less motivated, apathetic, and even angry
- Exerting less effort, producing lower quality work and even burning out
- Losing productivity, leading to less profitability

Research on incivility in the workplace has found that mental and physical health, productivity, employee retention, customer relations, and so on all greatly suffer when work and social environments are uncivil and that uncivil behavior tends to spread throughout an organization if the behavior goes uncorrected. These behaviors can include sarcasm, disparaging remarks, and hostility that violates workplace norms of collegiality—the cooperative relationship of colleagues.[84] The negative effects on one's physiological and psychological health may make it more difficult to gain meaning from one's work and satisfy higher-level needs such as self-actualization, which is discussed in the next chapter.

Uncivil behavior occurs, in part, because the aggressor fails to see the ethical dimension of their actions. They may think what they are doing is good, but, in reality, they have ethical blind spots.

Ethical Blind Spots

Some research suggests that individuals are *boundedly ethical*, which means they do not always recognize the ethical dimensions of their decisions because they are subject to ethical blind spots.[85] *Ethical blind spots* are obstacles that prevent us from seeing unethical behavior. According to Ann Tenbrunsel, the David E. Gallo Professor of Business Ethics at the Mendoza College of Business at the University of Notre Dame, these gaps between our conception of ethical behavior and how we act occur because of implicit biases, temporal distances that separate us from an ethical dilemma, and decision biases that lead people to disregard and misevaluate others' ethical lapses.[86]

Implicit biases may manifest as preferential treatment of some people we like or know personally, with the outcome being unconscious discrimination against those who lack such ties. Promoting a subordinate because we like that person rather than based on performance is a form of unconscious discrimination that demonstrates our implicit biases.

Temporal distance from decisions with ethical dimensions can be another source of unintentional unethical behavior. This means time separates us from the ethical dilemma. This distance in time influences the extent to which people believe they will be able to follow their moral compass. For example, when we think about the future, from which time separates us, we are more likely to think of how we want to behave and to consider that we would apply our ethical values to future decisions. Accordingly, individuals overestimate the extent to which they will make ethical decisions in the future because when the future becomes now, it's not always so easy to behave ethically. Temporal inconsistencies can prevent us from being as ethical as we desire to be.[87] Tenbrunsel explains this by saying, "When we are predicting how we will behave, we are thinking abstractly. But, when we are actually making the decisions, we are thinking very concretely, looking at feasibility."[88]

A good example of temporal distance and decision bias is the actions taken by Betty Vinson, a former accountant at

WorldCom, during the largest financial fraud in U.S. history. Vinson always thought she'd act ethically in the future, but when her superiors pressured her to manipulate financial results, she allowed those influences to alter her behavior. She had ethical blind spots and was unable to see the ethical dimensions of her decisions as they occurred. Exhibit 2.3 provides some background information on the case, which is discussed further in the next section.

Exhibit 2.3

WorldCom Fraud

The late 1990s and early 2000s ushered in a period of pervasive financial fraud by many large public companies that were manipulating financial statement results to make them look better than they really were. These companies were under a great deal of pressure because financial analysts had projected earnings levels higher than they could have legitimately reached, so company finance professionals looked for ways to manage earnings and increase the bottom line through improper means.

One such fraud occurred at WorldCom, an internet company that had been growing rapidly. The $11 billion fraud at WorldCom was the largest in U.S. history. As the economy slowed, WorldCom and other companies such as Enron struggled to "make the numbers"—reach analysts' estimates—and accountants got caught up in the hype. One such accountant was Betty Vinson, a midlevel accounting manager at WorldCom.

Vinson was pressured by her superiors and Scott Sullivan, the chief financial officer at WorldCom, to go along with fraudulent accounting that took operating expenses out of net income and recorded them as assets. The result was to delay recording these expenditures as operating expenses until the assets were used up over time, a process known as depreciation.

Vinson was ultimately sentenced to five months in prison and five months of house arrest. Judge Barbara Jones, who sentenced Vinson, commented, "Ms. Vinson was among the least culpable members of the conspiracy at WorldCom. . . . Still, had Vinson refused to do what she was asked, it's possible this conspiracy might have been nipped in the bud."[89]

Writing for the International City/County Management Association (ICMA), the leading association of government professionals, Kevin Duggan provides helpful advice on how to deal with the blind spots that can create biased behaviors:[90]

- Work to counter your ethical blind spots by seriously reflecting on decisions you are making and by thoughtfully considering what ethical choices may be at play.

- Seek the opinion of others whose judgment you respect, who have nothing to lose or gain (from a decision) regarding a possible course of action.

- Recognize when you might be doing the wrong thing to accomplish an otherwise admirable goal.

Biases may lead us to ignore the unethical behaviors of others. For example, individuals may fail to notice corrupt behavior if it benefits them and they fail to recognize their own conflicts of interest. This is known as *motivated blindness*, when it's in the decision maker's best interests *not* to see the unethical behavior of others.[91] This occurred for Betty Vinson, who was afraid to go against her superiors for fear of losing her job and not being able to support her family.

Ethical Slippery Slope

The *ethical slippery slope* refers to a pattern of behavior in which small unethical infractions lead to more egregious behaviors over time that may then lead to unintended consequences. It often starts by agreeing to go along with something that is wrong and then having to cover it up by perpetuating the falsehood. Once an individual gets away with the small lies, it becomes easier to accept bigger lies in the future.

Falling down the slippery slope may occur out of misplaced loyalty, as in the case of Betty Vinson. Vinson went along with improper accounting to make her boss happy. Even though she came to realize what she did—committing fraud—was wrong, she remained silent in large part because she said nothing about the falsehood at the very beginning. It became very difficult for her to reverse course and reclaim the moral high road after covering up the fraudulent behavior for so long.

Slippery slope arguments also exist in our daily lives. Here are a few examples:

- Lying about your activities to a loved one may lead to cover-ups in the future to cover your accumulating number of lies.

- Stealing small amounts of money may lead to larger thefts if you are able to get away with the initial crimes.

- Cheating on a spouse and getting away with it by telling convincing lies may lead to more cheating and cover-ups in the future.

There are also slippery slope arguments for societal activities:

- Making the production and sale of marijuana legal will lead to the legalization of harder drugs down the line.

- Allowing physicians to prescribe a cocktail of drugs to assist in the suicide of patients dying from cancer will lead to allowing assisted suicide in other situations, such as when a person is so depressed they no longer want to live.

These slippery slope arguments are based on suppositions about the future. They may or may not happen. The idea is to warn the decision maker that a certain kind of behavior at the present can lead to worse behavior in the future and have seriously negative effects.

Why Good People Sometimes Do Bad Things

Vinson's story also illustrates why good people sometimes do bad things. It doesn't mean they are bad people. Instead, circumstances may arise where the ethical aspects of a decision disappear from view and the moral implications are obscured, a concept known as *ethical fading*.[92]

Why did ethical fading occur in Vinson's case? It was caused by a form of *self-deception* or being unaware of the processes that led her to form opinions and judgments that were ethically improper. According to Sissela Bok, a Swedish-born American philosopher and ethicist, such deception involves avoidance of truth and the lies that we tell ourselves to keep our secrets.[93] Essentially, Vinson sought to rationalize what she was doing by overlooking what she knew to be improper accounting, reasoning that her boss must know better than she what was an acceptable practice, and buying in to her boss's claim that it was a one-time request. It rarely works that way and didn't for Vinson. Time and again she was pressured to do the same thing. She became more uncomfortable each time but didn't feel she could say no. She had compromised her values and believed her job and benefits might be at stake if she didn't continue to go along.

Had Vinson taken the time to identify the ethical issues first, not after the fact, and then to identify the values that were at stake, she may have made the right choice and not gone along with the fraud because she would have been more in touch with her ethical self.

Bystander Effect

The bystander effect was front and center in the Harvey Weinstein affair that has become synonymous with sexual abuse of women in Hollywood and the catalyst for the #MeToo movement that spread virally in October 2017 as a hashtag on social media to bring attention to the far-reaching effects of sexual assault and harassment, especially in the workplace. Exhibit 2.4 briefly summarizes the facts of the case.

How was it that so many actresses remained silent about the sexual innuendos and advances by Weinstein over such a long period of time, reportedly dating back to 1997? By all accounts, these women said nothing to prevent damage to their careers given the influence Weinstein had as a Hollywood producer. No one came forward; not the abused actresses, Hollywood agents, other producers, or even Brad Pitt and other actors who knew about it. In a real way, the silence was caused by the hope that others would disclose Weinstein's offensive behaviors (thus suffering the ill effects on their own careers). Thus, the bystander effect masked the ethical sensibilities of all the bystanders who failed to speak up or protest.

Exhibit 2.4

Harvey Weinstein Affair

Since 2017, when news broke that famed producer Harvey Weinstein had made unwanted sexual advances to Hollywood A-listers, such as Gwyneth Paltrow and Selma Hayek, eighty women have come forward to publicly accuse Weinstein of unwanted advances. Weinstein was charged with rape and sex abuse in cases involving three women. He pleaded not guilty to the charges. These cases are still pending.

The allegations of sexual assault in the Weinstein case motivated women in other fields to go public as well and to tell their stories of rape and sexual assault. These disclosures snowballed the #MeToo movement internationally, which shined a bright light on sexual harassment and sexual assault of women. In many cases, the egregious acts were perpetrated based on actual or implied conditions of advancing a woman's career. The power imbalance between Weinstein and many emerging actresses was the underlying factor that enabled his behavior.

Rationalizations

Rationalizations are explanations we tell ourselves and others for behaving improperly. "Everyone does it" is a common rationalization for unethical actions. In other words, everyone commits the unethical act and remains silent, so I'll do the same.

Another common rationalization is "if it isn't illegal, it's ethical." Writing on his Business Ethics blog, Chris MacDonald provides three examples of this type of faulty reasoning:[94]

1. Most kinds of lying are perfectly legal, but lying is generally considered to be unethical.

2. Breaking promises is generally legal but is widely thought of as unethical.

3. Cheating on a spouse is legal, but most people would consider it unethical.

Most people would probably admit that cheating on a spouse is unethical even though it breaks no laws because it does break vows of faithfulness. Yet, according to a 2018 study by General Social Survey, 20 percent of men and 13 percent of women reported that they've had sex with someone other than their spouse while married.[95] Why the disconnect? Most likely it's because of rationalizing behavior, such as thinking "my spouse cheated on me, so it's okay," or "we're in a loveless relationship and I deserve to be loved." This amounts to pursuing one's selfish interests and finding some way to explain it away.

Rationalizations are also used to avoid lying directly to spare someone's feelings by skirting the real question. For example, assume your wife comes home and puts on a new dress that you believe is unflattering and then asks for your opinion on how it looks. You don't want to hurt her feelings, but to avoid lying, you might say something like, "I like the colors of the dress."

We might also rationalize by telling a *white lie*, something said to avoid hurting another's feelings. Say your son builds a model spaceship for a class project and asks your opinion on how good it is. You don't want him to be upset by the truth, which is it's not as good as he can do, so you say something like, "I like it."

Small lies that are rationalized can become bigger lies later on, so it's best not to take the first step down the ethical slippery slope. More will be said about white lies in Chapter 3.

Examples of Practicing Ethical Behavior

The following brief scenarios provide an opportunity for you to apply the skills discussed earlier to resolve the given ethical dilemma.

1. Is it unfair to move to better seats at a sporting event when those seats are unoccupied?

Many people change their seats when more desirable seats are unoccupied. We move into an empty row in an airplane to have more space or to get off the plane more quickly. At sporting events, we move down to a lower section to have a better view of the playing field. Is it "cheating" to do so?

Most people would probably say no, because no one is directly harmed and everyone on the plane or in the stadium had an equal opportunity to do the same thing. The logic here may be summed up as "no harm, no foul."

Changing seats at a sporting event can make it more enjoyable. It seems to be a benign action as long as you are prepared to move back if asked to do so by the usher or seat holders.

2. You paid the bill at a restaurant in cash. The server gave you $10 more in change than he should have. Is it unfair to keep the extra $10?

Keeping the money is a selfish act. You may be motivated by greed or because you know you can get away with it. It's been said that ethics is about what we do when no one is looking. This is a good example. Would you act differently if you were out to dinner with your children and they noticed you kept the extra $10? What message do you want to send? This is an opportunity to set a high standard for your kids.

Also, consider that the server may get in trouble when

the cash tally is matched against the receipts for the day. Moreover, you do not deserve the $10. It's like stealing money. The Golden Rule is instructive here: What if you were the server? Wouldn't you want the customer to point out your mistake?

3. You are in a long line to buy a ticket at the movie theater. While you are distracted, someone cuts into the line in front of you. What would you do?

Cutting in line is a selfish act because it shows a disregard for another person. You might reason: I wouldn't cut in line in front of someone else, so I shouldn't blindly accept it when it is done to me. Perhaps the more important question is what you would do about it? You could try to reason with the other party. Maybe they apologize, maybe not. Expressing that you think it was wrong to cut in line shows courage. But it might provoke an argument. Are you ready for that?

Is it ever a good idea to let someone go in front of you? Yes, if they are pregnant, disabled, perhaps with a small child. These are thoughtful acts on your part. Some people in a supermarket with a full cart will allow the person behind them to go first if that person has only a small number of items. These are random acts of kindness. They occur on the spot. They're likely to be met with gratitude, which makes us feel better about ourselves. They may seem like little acts, but those add up as we practice them every day.

4. The lines at the supermarket are long, so you use the self-checkout scanner. You realize you forgot your credit cards and don't have enough cash to pay for everything. You're buying a lot of fruit and have to key in the type of fruit to ring up the price. The fruit you selected is organic, which costs about 20 percent more than nonorganic. The difference can save you enough to pay for all the food. Would you key in nonorganic fruit to save some money?

In all likelihood, no one would know if you keyed in nonorganic fruit and left the store. However, doing so to save money to pay for everything is rationalizing an unethical act. Remember, ethics is about what we do when no one is looking. Some scanner scammers might reason: "No one will get hurt: I'm cheating a faceless entity." However, this is like stealing from the store. A universality perspective is instructive here. Imagine if everyone did the same thing. The result may be that the supermarket raises prices for all. The danger for the individual is once they get away with it, similar actions may occur down the line, such as keying in a lesser quantity purchased. One wrong act begets another and the slippery slope phenomenon arises.

5. You just got your car insurance policy renewal information and the premium went up 20 percent because of thefts in your area. Your teenage son just started driving your car. You know you should inform the insurance company, but that might raise your premium another 20 percent. Would you inform the insurance company?

If you are an otherwise ethical person but decide not to inform the insurance company because of cost considerations, the act would fall into the category of why good people sometimes do bad things. Your action is not motivated by good intentions; it's self-serving. Some people in this situation might rationalize that their son is a safe driver and won't get into an accident, so there's no need to inform the company. But think about what might happen if your son does get into an accident and has not been included on your policy. Remember, ethical decision making requires a long-term perspective of right versus wrong.

In some cases, a car insurance policy may not cover family members living in your home unless they are specifically named on your policy. A compounding ethical issue is if you've deceived the insurance company, and your son is in an accident, it could lead to a more difficult claims process or voiding of your policy. Of course, these are not the primary reasons to include your son as a driver—it's to do the right thing. In other words, the end of saving money on your insurance does not justify the means of omitting important information from your insurance application that the company has a right to know. Moreover, what message are you sending your teenage son by failing to disclose information that the insurance company has a right to know?

6. You pulled out of a tight space in a parking lot and dented the car next to you. You're not sure if anyone saw you. What would you do?

It shouldn't matter whether someone witnessed what you did or not. If you reason that it does, then you're using ethical relativism to rationalize what's appropriate in the situation. Let's examine how the ethical decision-making process described in Figure 1.1 in Chapter 1 might help to analyze the ethical issues involved. Here is a brief review of the process as it relates to this decision.

Decision-Making Process

Ethical Awareness

Recognize the ethical issues

Should you report denting the other car given you're at fault?

Identify the ethical values

- *Honesty:* Concealing information about the accident is untruthful; a lie by omission.

- *Responsibility:* You made a mistake and should own up to it; be accountable for your actions.

Ethical Judgment

Identify and analyze the alternatives

Whether you should leave a note with contact information for the driver, report it to the police, or do nothing at all. We'll use utilitarianism and deontology to analyze the ethics of the alternatives.

1. Leave contact information or report your mistake.

Benefits:

- If you report it, you can get your car fixed minus the deductible and your insurance will cover damage to the other's car.

- You won't get in trouble if someone saw you and, perhaps, took down your license plate and reported the incident.

- You avoid leaving the scene of an accident. In most states you need to make a reasonable effort to identify the owner of the vehicle and notify them about what happened. If you are unable to find the owner, you should leave a written notice with your contact information.

Harms/Costs:

- Even if no one saw the accident, by considering not reporting it you are creating problems for yourself when it isn't necessary to do so (rationalizing an unethical act).

- Your insurance premium will likely increase.

2. Don't leave contact information or report the dent.

Benefits:

- If no one saw you, there is no risk it would be reported (assuming the parking lot does not have cameras that may have taken a picture of the accident).

- If no one saw you, there will be no out-of-pocket expenses unless you choose to fix the car and cover the deductible.

- If no one saw you, the insurance premium will not go up.

Harms/Costs:

- If someone saw you, they might take down your license plate and report it to the police. Now you have violated the motor vehicle laws by not reporting the accident.

- If someone saw you, a police investigation may ensue for leaving the scene of an accident.

- If someone saw you, expect an increase in the insurance premium as you work through the details with your insurance carrier.

- Even if no one saw you, failing to leave your contact information or notify the police gets you on the slippery slope of having to cover up your failure to notify, deceive others, and failure to take responsibility.

From a utilitarian perspective, more harms than benefits will occur if you don't report the accident. You are risking severe penalties if you are caught. Moreover, not reporting the accident can be characterized as a cowardly act in which fear and excessive self-concern override doing what is right, good, and of help to others in time of need. Most important, since ethics is doing the right thing even when no one is looking, failing to act means you lack the ethical character necessary to be a virtuous person—at least in this case.

Ethical Intent

Decide on a course of action

This is based on the ethical analysis. Ethical intent is important. Recall that Kant addresses the importance of good will. He conceived of virtue as the strength or will to fulfill one's duties despite any opposing inclinations. We should do what is right because we are motivated to do the right thing and not let our selfish interests to avoid responsibility get in the way. Applying the Kantian universality perspective, we should act in ways we would will others to act in similar situations for similar reasons. We would want the other driver to contact us if they had hit our car. We have a moral duty not to harm others or their property.

Ethical Action

Check yourself

Applying the "checking yourself" step in the decision-making process, we could ask what we would do if our son or daughter were in our car when we dented the other car. We presumably wouldn't want our son or daughter to witness the accident and us doing nothing about it. What kind of example would that be setting? Would you be proud of your action? How would you want others to act if the roles were reversed?

Behave ethically

Carry out ethical intent with ethical action.

Though not completely analogous, deciding what to do when you dent a car in a parking lot does trigger an automatic response. As previously mentioned, Gentile points out that we can call upon our moral muscle memory to guide our reaction once our physiological and psychological states are aroused.[96] If we have encountered similar situations in the past, then we can actually develop default behavior, which should be to report the matter and accept responsibility for our actions.

How Living Ethically or Unethically Can Change Lives

Our actions define who we are and what we stand for. They are major contributors to the reputation we gain for honesty, integrity, and trustworthiness or the absence thereof. It may seem that happiness can be achieved by taking advantage of others without their knowledge in order to enrich oneself. The case of Michael Milken illustrates just that. It also shows how someone who did a bad thing managed to reverse course and become a respected member of the community, in part because of his philanthropic activities. So, the message of this chapter is that you can become an ethical person, or a more ethical person, if you commit to doing so, act in accordance with ethical intentions, and apply the tools in this book to practice making ethical decisions.

Michael Milken: The Resurrection

Can a person recover from committing a highly unethical act? Is it possible to transform from villain to hero? It would appear so, even though it is not very common. One example of turning it around is Michael Milken.

Milken became known as the king of junk bonds in the 1970s and 1980s. These were bonds issued by companies with low credit ratings that had difficulty raising funds. Milken convinced these companies to sell the bonds by offering a higher interest rate to investors to induce them to buy the risky bonds. He made capital available to lots of individuals and lots of institutions that otherwise would not have had access. Believing that the rewards outweighed the likelihood that his customers would be unable to pay interest and repay debt, he advised bond issuers and investors to take full advantage of them, hence setting junk bonds ablaze in popularity and seeming success.

Milken was seen as a poster child for corporate greed. U.S. District Court judge Kimba Wood told him at his sentencing hearing: "When a man of your power in the financial world . . . repeatedly conspires to violate, and violates, securities and tax business in order to achieve more power and wealth for himself . . . a significant prison term is required." Milken was sentenced to ten years in prison (later reduced to two years).[97]

Exhibit 2.5 provides background information on Milken's

prison sentence and subsequent activities that helped turn his reputation for unabashed greed into one of a generous philanthropist.

Exhibit 2.5

The Saga of Michael Milken

Milken became successful in part because the financial markets were deregulated in 1986, reducing the controls that might have cut down on the risky junk bond investments he promoted to unsuspecting investors. In April 1990, after four years of investigation for these risky practices and insider trading, Milken was indicted on ninety-eight counts of racketeering and securities fraud and agreed to plead guilty to criminal violation of securities laws and to pay a $600 million fine.

Following his early release from prison, Milken turned to reinventing himself through charitable endeavors, including the Milken Family Foundation, which has raised more than $660 million and provided funding to more than two thousand research projects at more than two hundred cancer centers and universities in nineteen countries around the world. Thanks to Milken, some twenty-three "chemically distinct" anti–prostate cancer medicines have been developed. A 2004 *Fortune* cover story hailed Milken as "the man who changed medicine." Milken came to the ethical life after not regarding it highly, and it influenced others to think more positively about him given the benefits of his actions to society.[98]

For thirty years, the Milken Educator Awards, an initiative of the Milken Family Foundation, have rewarded and inspired excellence in the world of education by honoring top educators around the country with $25,000 in unrestricted awards. Not an accolade for "lifetime achievement" or the proverbial gold watch at the exit door, the Milken Educator Awards target early- to midcareer education professionals for their already impressive achievements and, more significantly, for the promise of what they will accomplish in the future. To date, more than 2,700 awards have been given out, totaling $68 million.

Author and former Wall Street investment banker Michael Thomas calls Milken's personal narrative one of "the great reversals": empowerment through disempowerment, when you become disempowered in one sphere but empowered and almost as influential in another.[99]

Opinions about Milken vary from believing he is an opportunist to a philanthropist. What's clear is he sought greater meaning in life through his charitable activities, perhaps because of the guilt he felt for scamming investors. We might explain it by asking: What motivates a person to transform their life and become ethical? In Milken's case, it seems in prison he reflected on his actions and realized he had done bad things and needed to make amends. By all accounts, Milken went from being someone who pursued self-interest regardless of the cost to others to someone who genuinely wanted to help others.

The moral of the story is we can change our behaviors by learning the art of ethical behavior and applying it to everyday life. Like Michael Milken, gaining self-respect and self-esteem can enhance our well-being if we are able to overcome the blind spots that once made it difficult to clearly distinguish between right and wrong.

Conclusion

Ethical behavior is an ongoing activity. It's not like a faucet you can turn on or off at a whim. You can enhance your well-being by consistently making right, not wrong, decisions, by doing good, not bad, things. Acting this way enhances our ethical sense. One way to think of ethics is as a blueprint for doing things that improve the lives of others and bring happiness and greater meaning to your life through practice and repetition. In the next chapter, you will learn just how this comes about.

CHAPTER 3

The Pursuit of Happiness and Meaning

Happiness is not something ready-made. It comes from your own actions.

—The Dalai Lama

The Dalai Lama is the spiritual leader of Tibet. His statement means that happiness is the result of the kind of person you are, the decisions you make, the consequences of your actions for others, and whether you meet your responsibilities to a moral society.

A happy life is one in which we are satisfied with our circumstances, and a meaningful life is one in which we take steps to achieve our purpose. Our happiness can be strengthened through living a life of meaning, allowing us to flourish. We can transform our lives and gain happiness and greater meaning by knowing what promotes these ends and how to ethically deal with the factors that make happiness and meaning more difficult to achieve.

We pursue happiness and meaning to lead fulfilling lives and enhance our well-being. We pursue happiness through relationships with others; happiness comes from external activities. Through our relationships with others, we can build mutual respect. We pursue meaning through actions we take for our own growth and development and to better the lives of others. These actions can build self-esteem. By understanding the reasons why we pursue happiness and meaning and how we can do so successfully, we are better equipped to develop the ethical means to achieve life's goals.

Respecting others strengthens relationships and can create an environment that fosters civility in our lives. Being kind, attentive to the needs of others, and trustworthy are behaviors that promote civility. Treating others with civility opens up the possibility of developing meaningful relationships that can advance our mutual interests, and meaningful relationships can build self-esteem and make us happy as a result. They can also lead to satisfying higher-level needs, such as self-actualization (discussed later in this chapter). Once we have reached a level of self-actualization, or have achieved our full potential, we can turn our attention to helping others achieve a higher purpose and contribute to the betterment of society.

Knowing our purpose in life is important to our happiness because it grounds our behavior. Our purpose is the central motivating factor that gets us up in the morning—our reason for being—and meaning is the value we assign to that belief. Because it has a value orientation, meaning in life has an ethical component to it.

As discussed in Chapter 1, learning the art of ethical behavior can advance our happiness and the meaningfulness of our lives by allowing us to develop moral and intellectual virtues that strengthen our character and enable us to meet our end goals in life. If we are to achieve happiness in life, we need to treat others the way we wish they would treat us and expect them to do the same. We also need to consider how our actions affect others. If we are to achieve meaning in life, our actions should be worthwhile and accompanied by a sense of value in our accomplishments.[100] We should engage in activities that are fulfilling.

Historically, the nature and pursuit of happiness and meaning have been addressed through two opposing philosophical traditions: the hedonic and the eudaimonic. The *hedonic* perspective suggests that happiness can be achieved by maximizing one's pleasurable moments: seeking pleasure, avoiding pain. Well-being, in this sense, is associated with emotional states that accompany desire; therefore, experiences of pleasure, carefreeness, and enjoyment reflect well-being.[101]

Eudaimonic well-being involves having a sense of purpose, setting and achieving goals, and feeling what you do in life is worthwhile. Aristotle thought that true happiness was found by leading a virtuous life and doing what was worth doing. He believed that realizing human potential is the ultimate human goal.[102] Conceptually, both approaches contribute to happiness and meaning—human flourishing. Research suggests that a life rich in both corresponds with the highest degree of well-being.[103]

Before we discuss happiness and meaning in life in more depth, it's important to understand what well-being is.

What Is Well-Being?

Tchiki Davis, founder of the Berkeley Well-Being Institute at the University of California, characterizes well-being as the experience of health, happiness, and prosperity. It includes having good mental health, high life satisfaction, and a sense of meaning or purpose.[104]

Davis identifies five types of well-being that can be enhanced by applying skills.[105] These are emotional, physical, social, workplace, and societal well-being. See Table 3.1.

Table 3.1
Skills Needed to Develop Well-Being

Type of Well-Being	Skills
Emotional well-being	Practice stress management, be resilient, and generate the emotions that lead to good feelings.
Physical well-being	Improve the functioning of your body through healthy eating and exercise.
Social well-being	Communicate well with others, develop meaningful relationships, and maintain a support network to counteract loneliness.
Workplace well-being	Pursue your interests, values, and purpose in order to gain meaning, happiness, and enrichment professionally.
Societal well-being	Actively participate in a thriving community, culture, and environment.

Physical well-being has been defined by the American Association of Nurse Anesthetists as "the lifestyle behavior choices you make to ensure health, avoid preventable diseases and conditions, and live in a balanced state of mind and spirit." It is closely connected to emotional or *mental well-being*, which deals with how you are feeling and how well you can cope with day-to-day life.

Davis points out that to build one's overall well-being all the types of well-being must be functioning, to an extent. For example, if you haven't developed stress management skills or coping mechanisms, you're less likely to develop meaningful relationships and thus your social well-being may lag. Well-being is a dynamic concept and our well-being can change from moment to moment, day to day, month to month, or year to year. According to a mental health organization in the United Kingdom called Mind.org, good mental well-being enables us to do the following:[106]

- Feel relatively confident in ourselves and have positive self-esteem
- Feel and express a range of emotions
- Build and maintain good relationships with others
- Feel engaged with the world around us
- Live and work productively
- Cope with the stresses of daily life
- Adapt and manage in times of change and uncertainty

Davis identifies practicing skills like gratitude, kindness, and communication to enhance social well-being because they facilitate positive interactions with others and help us feel more meaningfully connected to others.

Gratitude can be a simple "thank you" to someone who has helped us, but, on a deeper level, it is showing appreciation for someone or something, which produces a more long-lasting positive feeling. Gratitude is not just an action but also an emotion that serves a purpose. Showing gratitude can help build stronger relationships and a sense of belonging. Gratitude acts are done unconditionally to show appreciation and not in anticipation of receiving something in return, although the recipient may return the favor at an appropriate time and, perhaps, pay it forward, as discussed in Chapter 2.[107]

Unlike the five types of well-being discussed above, psychological well-being deals with the mind and human behavior. Carol Ryff, known for her research on psychological well-being, identifies six factors that contribute to an individual's psychological well-being, contentment, and happiness. The six factors are self-acceptance, positive relations with others, a sense of autonomy in thought and action, the ability to manage complex environments to suit personal needs, the pursuit of meaningful goals and a sense of purpose in life, and continued growth and development as a person.[108] These factors are linked to Maslow's hierarchy of needs and the notion of self-actualization—the feeling of having achieved something in one's life—that are discussed later. For now, Table 3.2 describes each of the six factors.

Table 3.2
Psychological Well-Being

Type of Psychological Well-Being	Description
Self-acceptance	A characteristic of self-actualization, optimal functioning, and maturity
Positive relations with others	Strong feelings of empathy and affection for all human beings
Autonomy	Self-determination, independence, and the regulation of behavior from within

Environmental mastery	Ability to choose and create environments that enable one to advance in the world and change it creatively through physical or mental activities
Purpose in life	Beliefs that give one the feeling there is purpose in and meaning to life, a sense of directedness, and intentionality
Personal growth	Going beyond achieving the first five characteristics to continue to develop one's potential, to grow and expand as a person

Martin Seligman, the father of Positive Psychology, which deals with the study of happiness and other positive aspects and experiences in life, wrote about the role of positive emotions as indicators of flourishing and optimal well-being. According to Seligman, positive emotion is a subjective variable, characterized by what we think and feel.[109] Unlike objective well-being, which can be measured by tracking (and later aggregating) people's momentary experiences of good and bad feelings, subjective well-being deals with one's cognitive and affective evaluations of life.[110] Experiencing positive emotion can bring "joy, interest, contentment, love, and the like . . . moments not plagued by negative emotions such as anxiety, sadness, anger, and despair. Consistent with this intuition, the overall balance of people's positive and negative emotions has been shown to predict their judgments of subjective well-being."[111]

Subjective well-being is the scientific term for happiness and life satisfaction—thinking and feeling that your life is going well, not badly. The science of well-being doesn't tell us what should make people happy. It aims to tell us what *does* make people happy. It suggests that along with experiencing good feelings, people need to undertake activities that are meaningful and engaging and that make them feel competent and autonomous. Multiple studies in Positive Psychology point to self-actualization as a component of well-being.[112] As you will see, self-actualization is thought to be crucial to leading a happy life filled with meaning, one in which we thrive.

What Is Thriving?

A person who is thriving is high in well-being and their life is functioning. They can bounce back quickly from problems, take advantage of new opportunities, and feel good and strong physically, mentally, and socially. This is what researchers mean by *thriving*.[113]

In a review of the existing literature, Daniel Brown, PhD, and fellow researchers characterize thriving as: "an individual experiencing a sense of development, of getting better at something, and succeeding at mastering something. In the simplest terms, what underpins it is feeling good about life and yourself and being good at something."[114]

Brooke Feeney and Nancy Collins identify five aspects of thriving in their research study on thriving through relationships:[115]

- Happiness, life satisfaction, subjective well-being (hedonic well-being)

- Having purpose and meaning in life and progressing toward meaningful goals; movement toward full potential (eudaimonic well-being)

- Feeling good about oneself; self-acceptance (psychological well-being)

- Deep and meaningful human connections; positive interpersonal expectations (social well-being)
- Mental and emotional well-being (physical well-being)

Much of thriving is about engaging in meaningful activities and relationships that make us feel better about ourselves (they build self-esteem), fulfill our higher needs for growth and to be all that we can be, achieve our purpose in life (self-actualization), and go beyond ourselves and what we are capable of and improve the lives of others (transcendence).

Life coaches Don Nenninger and Nicole Nenninger believe thriving brings more happiness and fulfillment into our lives; when we thrive we live a better life. They describe twenty practices, ten of which are listed below.[116] I chose these ten because they are relevant to learning the art of ethical behavior.

1. Practice gratitude on a daily basis until it becomes a habit.

2. Choose your thoughts carefully. Check yourself before acting.

3. Take care of your body.

4. Look for beauty and inspiration to guide you in life.

5. Forgive yourself and others for past "mistakes": learn from your experiences and move on.

6. Learn how to disagree respectfully.

7. Pay attention to your limiting beliefs that may hold you back from pursuing meaningful relationships.

8. Give back to the world in a positive manner.

9. Learn to be 100 percent responsible for your life.

10. Have a purpose in life, something that has value and that can enhance your well-being.

Writing about the relationship between happiness and well-being for Thrive Global, an organization that promotes well-being, Ryan Bronson characterizes happiness as a state of emotional well-being.[117] He asserts that happiness can exist without well-being, but well-being can't exist without happiness. Happiness is also one of the factors of psychological well-being because it makes us feel that our lives are going well. Thriving enhances well-being because it enables growth and development that brings emotional well-being. We thrive through relationships that create happiness and activities that advance meaning in life.

What Is Happiness?

His Holiness the Dalai Lama is known for his moral writings and speeches, including those on achieving happiness. The Dalai Lama believes happiness is the end goal in life: "The very purpose of our existence is to seek happiness." In his book *The Art of Happiness*, the Dalai Lama links happiness more to our state of mind than to our external conditions, circumstances, or events—after our basic survival needs are met—and says that happiness can be achieved through the systematic training of our hearts and minds.[118] (See Exhibit 3.1 to learn more about the Dalai Lama.)

The desire for happiness is in everyone's nature, according to the Dalai Lama. Happiness is found through love, affection, closeness, and compassion. Sharing feelings and expressing ourselves with the expectation of not being judged enhances our physical and mental well-being. Aristotle was convinced that a genuinely happy life required the fulfillment of a broad range of conditions, including physical and mental well-being.

Exhibit 3.1

His Holiness the Dalai Lama

His Holiness the 14th Dalai Lama, Tenzin Gyatso, is a Buddhist monk and the spiritual leader of Tibet, an autonomous region of China. In 1940, he was enthroned as the Dalai Lama but it wasn't until 1950, at the age of fifteen, that he was called upon to assume full political power after China invaded and seized control of Tibet. He remained in that position until 2011, when steps toward democratization created political institutions to run the country. He announced that he was ending the custom by which the Dalai Lamas exercised political authority in Tibet but continued to lead the country in spiritual affairs.

The Dalai Lama is globally recognized as a man of peace. He has traveled to more than sixty-seven countries spanning six continents spreading his message of peace and compassion and promoting interreligious harmony and understanding. In 1989, he was awarded the Nobel Peace Prize for his nonviolent struggle for the liberation of Tibet.[119]

John Helliwell, author of the *2017 World Happiness Report*, stated his opinion that people are more likely to be happy as a reward for a life well lived. This was based on the responses of three thousand people asked to assess their lives and how their relationships with others promoted happiness. The report identified factors that support happiness, including trust (no. 1): people tend to trust each other; quality of work experience (no. 5): people have a healthy relationship to work, that is, high levels of autonomy and job quality; civil society (no. 7): a higher degree of socialization; and balance in life (no. 8): a balance between work and leisure.[120] These results reflect a state of mental well-being that is integral to happiness and contributes to greater meaning in life.

Are people generally happy? The *2019 World Happiness Report* shows that the United States is ranked nineteenth. Why so low? The report says it's because of a high level of addictions causing unhappiness and depression. "The compulsive pursuit of substance abuse and addictive behaviors is causing severe unhappiness."[121] The dangers of taking too much of any opioid was discussed in Chapter 1. The quick high from taking a pill creates a physical dependence that can lead to taking stronger opioids to maintain that feeling.

Which countries are the happiest? Basically, the Nordic countries—Finland, Norway, Denmark, Iceland. It appears the reasons these countries are at the top of the list is clean environment, feeling they are one with nature, and success at converting wealth into well-being. Some have said the reason for a high level of happiness in these countries is they practice a brand of "compassionate capitalism," where free-market economics, high taxes, and entitlement programs create a foundation for the betterment of society.[122]

For happiness to occur, we need to engage in activities that strengthen our mental well-being while we build habits of ethical behavior along the way. The following sections illustrate how living our lives based on ethical values can qualitatively improve our relationships with others, which leads to happiness.

Truth Telling

Most people know that honesty is about truth telling. But you may be less familiar with what some people do to obscure the truth through outright lies, omitting information, and distorting the facts. Others tell white lies and dismiss them as unimportant.

Lying is never a good thing because it raises questions about why anyone should believe what we say if we are a person known to lie. Lying can be deceitful and cause others to make unwise choices based on our words. Imagine that a friend who trusts you is about to get married and asks whether you've heard anything about their soon-to-be spouse cheating with another person. You know that cheating occurred but answer in the negative out of a sense of loyalty to your friend's partner, with whom you have a closer relationship. The marriage goes forward and soon thereafter the spouse cheats again.

You may have been able to prevent the hardship to your friend by being truthful. Here, you had to choose between the values of honesty and loyalty to another. Recall that both honesty and loyalty are components of one of the Josephson Institute's Six Pillars of Character—trustworthiness. Loyalty is an important value because it shows we have the interests of others at heart, but it's not blind loyalty that we are concerned with ethically but being faithful to commitments and obligations to others. Values sometimes conflict as here and, as a general rule, it's best not to let loyalties get in the way of honesty because there are all kinds of situations in which we could cover up the truth about wrongful actions in the name of loyalty, rationalizing the lying.

Let's look at the omission of information, a type of lying. Many people use dating apps to connect with other people. How would you feel if a person you met online failed to mention they were married? You'd probably feel disheartened once you found out. The omission of information can be just as harmful as telling an outright lie because it creates a sense of distrust. A lie by omission is just as wrong as a lie by commission, where you knowingly tell an untruth.

Distortions, another type of lying, occur when we alter the meaning of some fact or event. For example, assume a potential employer asks: "How many years of experience do you have in the field?" You overstate it by two years by interpreting the question as "any experience" even though the question asked for "experience in the field." That's a distortion of information, and it may come back to harm you if you are given a job you're not prepared for. Perhaps your boss puts you in charge of an assignment and you're not ready for it. All trust may be lost once your boss discovers your inability to do what you should have been able to do if you had the requisite amount of experience you claimed. This example illustrates the snowball effect of lying. A small lie takes on greater consequence over time.

White Lies

According to Merriam-Webster's online dictionary, a *white lie* is "a lie about a small or unimportant matter that someone tells to avoid hurting another person." According to Devon McDermott, a relationship psychologist, "The biggest problem with white lies is that we often need to continue to create more and more lies to cover the tracks of our original lies."[123] Thus, we begin the decline down the ethical slippery slope, where something said or done that may seem relatively harmless today leads to coverups in the future that have more serious consequences, and we risk lying becoming part of our character.

White lies can have a cumulative effect: you tell one small lie and get away with it and then are more likely to tell other lies later. Lying is a learned behavior. We might ask: Is it ever acceptable to tell a white lie? There are no rules of the game, although lifestyle reporter Wendy Rose Gould suggests that if a white lie requires additional white lies or hinders the expression of your personal needs, then you should tell the truth. She suggests delivering honesty "with a side of gentleness."[124] Here are three examples of when you should tell the truth and avoid the temptation to lie:

1. Someone from work asks you out for a date and you don't want to hurt his feelings, so you make up an excuse by saying you have other plans. This may seem like a small lie to prevent hurting your coworker's feelings, and you may even think it's best to lie to preserve workplace harmony. However, the way you responded opens the door for being asked out again. It's best to be honest to avoid having to lie again and again. You could explain that you don't think of the coworker in a romantic way but want to be friends. (Of course, don't say "friends" if you don't really mean it.)

2. You want to break off a relationship but don't want to hurt the other person's feelings. Staying in the relationship may cause more long-term harm than breaking it off as soon as you feel there's no longer a spark or you've met someone else or your feelings have changed. If you don't tell the other person, you're going to have to lie about wanting to go places together and do things together and spend time together. You don't help the other person by delaying the inevitable and making it seem like you're still interested. It's best to be blunt and tell the truth even though it might hurt their feelings.

3. You just started a new job and your boss explains your responsibilities. The explanation is confusing and you don't fully understand, yet when asked if you have

any questions, you say no because you don't want to come off as being dense or like you're accusing the boss of being unclear. This lie may affect your ability to do your job and do it well, so, instead, you should say something like, "I just want to be sure I got it all." Then ask your specific questions.

Let's be honest. There are times when a white lie seems to be the least offensive thing to say. How many of these white lies have you told?

1. Someone gives you a gift you don't like. Do you say you don't like it or something such as: "Thanks for the thoughtful gift"?

2. You're on a phone call with an acquaintance who goes on and on. You don't want to hurt his feelings but can't stand it any longer. Do you abruptly get off the phone or say something like: "I lost track of time and have to go now"?

3. A friend of yours calls and asks you to meet up with her and three others from work. You are currently at odds with one group member. You don't want to create undue stress for your friend or the other group members by explaining why you won't go. Do you say something like: "Thanks for asking, but I have other plans"?

The common thread in each of these situations is your desire to avoid making someone feel bad about what they said or did. It seems you'd be acting more compassionately if you were to set aside your true feelings for the benefit of another, and white lies seem reasonable under the circumstances.

The most important thing to remember is not to tell a lie

to avoid personal responsibility. If your boss asks whether you have completed an important project and you haven't, don't make up an excuse, such as "I got called away from my desk," just to avoid conflict. Explain why it's taking longer. There may be a good reason. Even if it's just a matter of you're working more slowly than anticipated, the worst thing to do is deny accountability. Accepting the consequences of our actions is a matter of integrity, a foundational value of a principled person.

Promise Keeping

When we make promises or other commitments that create a legitimate basis for another person to rely on us, we undertake distinctive moral duties. The act of making a promise implies an obligation to keep it. According to the Josephson Institute, promise keeping builds trustworthiness, and to keep promises, we should avoid the following behaviors:[125]

Avoid bad-faith excuses. Don't try to rationalize why you did not keep a promise because it may come across as an intent to deceive.

Your spouse asks why you didn't pick up the kids after school, as you had promised, so you make up an excuse that an important meeting came up and you lost track of time.

Avoid unwise commitments. Don't make promises that you're not willing to keep.

You're in a relationship with someone you care for deeply but don't share some of her interests. She loves to hike and bike up mountains, but you're a couch potato. She raises the issue and tells you it's an important matter for her, so you promise you'll become more outdoorsy. You're essentially agreeing to change your behavior even though you may have no intent to do so.

Avoid unclear communication. Be sure the other person understands what you are committing to. Avoid ambiguity, where more than one interpretation is possible.

In conversations in the past, your girlfriend has complained that you don't pay attention to her. You promise to try harder. Does this mean you'll be a better listener or more responsive to her needs?

When we don't keep a promise to someone, it communicates to that person that we don't value them, that we have chosen to put something else ahead of our commitment.[126] Imagine that you had agreed to study for an exam with a group of friends one night. They're depending on you to discuss some of the material on the test. However, that day your girlfriend calls and says she has two concert tickets for your favorite group. You want to go to the show, so you beg off your promise to the group by asking whether the study session could be delayed until the following morning. In addition to being inconsiderate of the group, you've jeopardized the trust of those friends because you made a promise that you were not willing to keep if a better offer came along. Your friends would start to wonder whether you are trustworthy.

Kindness

Kindness is defined as the quality of being warm, generous, and considerate. *Affection, concern, care,* and *empathy* are words that are associated with kindness.[127] Kindness and empathy are linked in that an unkind person probably does not understand another person's situation, that is, does not see things through the other's eyes and sense their feelings, the definition of empathy. An unkind person isn't concerned with the well-being of others, at least not as much as they should be to practice ethical behavior.

It is difficult to imagine having a satisfying relationship without honesty and kindness because these qualities build trust in relationships. Kindness has been found by researchers to be the most important predictor of stability in a marriage. It is the glue that keeps two people together.[128] The Love Lab experiment described in Exhibit 3.2 explains why kindness is so important to a happy relationship.

Exhibit 3.2

The Love Lab Experiment

In 1986, psychologist John Gottman and his colleague Robert Levinson began an experiment in what they called the Love Lab. They brought together newlyweds and watched them interact with each other.

Over time, they learned that the number one factor that breaks up marriages is when spouses focus on criticizing their partners and, rather than seeing the positive things their partners are doing, see negativity when it's not there. People who deliberately ignore their partner or respond minimally damage the relationship by making their partner feel worthless and invisible, as if they are not there, not valued.

On the other hand, kindness is the most important predictor of satisfaction and stability in a marriage. Kindness makes each partner feel cared for, understood, and validated—feel loved. The researchers conclude that kindness must be practiced all of the time, especially during fights, when feelings of contempt and aggression can spiral out of control and cause irrevocable harm.[129]

A blog post on the website Becoming Who You Are states that sometimes kindness means saying no, such as when saying yes would enable bad behavior. What would you do if a friend asks for money, spends it on drugs, and then asks for more money to perpetuate the habit? You would be enabling bad behavior if you continue to give your friend money. It's kinder to refuse when a person is struggling with unhealthy behaviors or patterns and let them face the consequences of their action.[130] This is a version of tough love. It may not bring happiness to you, but it can add meaning to your life by helping others in need.

Compassion

Compassion has been defined in many ways. Merriam-Webster's online dictionary defines it as "sympathetic consciousness of others' distress together with a desire to alleviate it." In the literature, there appears to be a broad consensus that compassion involves feeling for a person who is suffering and being motivated to act to help them.[131] According to the Theosophical Society of America, the characteristic trait compassion lies at the heart of all religious, ethical, and spiritual traditions, directing us always to treat others as we wish to be treated ourselves.[132]

Compassion is sometimes differentiated from empathy and altruism, although the concepts are related. *Empathy* refers more generally to our ability to take the perspective of and feel the emotions of another person, and *compassion* is when those feelings and thoughts include the desire to help them. *Altruism*, in turn, is the kind, selfless behavior often motivated by feelings of compassion, though one can feel compassion without acting on it, and altruism isn't always motivated by compassion.[133] It could simply be that a person sees helping others as a way to add meaning to their life.

Research by Martin Seligman suggests that connecting with others in a meaningful way helps us enjoy better mental and physical health. A compassionate lifestyle leads to greater psychological health because giving to others is a pleasurable activity, if not more so than the act of receiving. It also broadens our perspective beyond ourselves and creates a sense of connection to others that generates a positive feeling and enhances well-being.[134]

Empathy and compassion for others may be reciprocated. For example, let's assume your next-door neighbor's husband just died and you decide to cook some meals and bring them over so the family can grieve without worrying about the little things. Six months later, your husband passes away and your neighbor returns the favor. One good deed deserves another. We feel good about what we did and our neighbor's actions. It gives us a sense of satisfaction and gratitude, two elements of happiness.

Integrity

Integrity refers to the wholeness of a person, one's character. It is the quality of being honest, reliable, and trustworthy. A person with integrity lives according to moral principles and is willing to stand up and do the right thing even if there are personal costs; they have moral courage. For example, people who blow the whistle on wrongdoing are willing to jeopardize their work position to do the right thing regardless of the consequences to themselves.

I was once faced with that exact situation and remember the agony I went through deciding on the proper course of action. One day I discovered that the head of the Accounting Department at the university where I taught had plagiarized material in a research paper. My ethical dilemma was what to do with this information.

I weighed the pros and cons. It was clear the plagiarism violated academic integrity and I had a moral duty to report it. However, the department head was a friend of mine and responsible for my hiring. I was torn between being honest and being loyal to my friend. I could have forgotten about it, figuring no one else would find out.

It took some time and thought, but I "checked myself," as suggested in the decision-making process described in Figure 1.1 in Chapter 1, by quickly focusing on the important issue: How would I feel if my decision made it to the front pages of the *Chronicle of Higher Education*, a publication devoted to discussing issues in academia? Would I be proud of it? How might my friends and family feel about it? I surely wouldn't have felt proud if the *Chronicle* reported that I knew about academic dishonesty, had a chance to do something about it, but didn't.

I reported the matter to the dean, who told me there had been other complaints. He relieved the department head of his responsibilities but didn't fire him for cause.

Looking back, I felt a sense of relief in reporting the department head. I had been living with the knowledge he cheated the system and it was unfair to the rest of us who had academic integrity. I can't say I was happy about it but did feel more valued for what I did.

It's important to know what promotes happiness in life, and it's just as important to understand what makes happiness more difficult to achieve so that you know what to avoid.

What Prevents Happiness in Life?

Jesse Stuart, a consultant on health and wellness, identifies ten factors that hold us back from being happy. These include: (1) fear of change; (2) postponing happiness till the future; (3) comparing our lives to others who have more; (4) looking outside ourselves for happiness; (5) unrealistic expectations/perfectionism; (6) negative thoughts; (7) not living in the present; (8) being too busy to stop and smell the roses; (9) not being grateful for what we have; and (10) not enjoying the journey because of overemphasizing the end goal.[135]

Space does not permit discussing all of these factors in detail, and most are self-evident. Briefly, when we look outside ourselves for happiness, the inner state of our character is relegated to a secondary position and we let others define what happiness looks like. For example, if we are in an unfulfilling relationship—that is, an unfulfilling relationship in which our emotional needs are not met—our pursuit of happiness may be stifled and we are left picking up the pieces of a failed relationship.

Sometimes we get caught up in unsatisfying relationships that we did not anticipate. Behaviors linked to internet and social media use, such as trolling and ghosting, can bring unhappiness. A more serious behavior online is cyberbullying. Cyberbullying is a form of incivility that can do real damage to the person being bullied by injuring their self-esteem to the point where they harm themselves.

The Cyberbullying Research Center defines *cyberbullying* as willful and repeated harm inflicted through the use of computers, cell phones, and other electronic devices.[136] Cyberbullying is different from bullying because a certain amount of anonymity is associated with it. Someone on a social networking site can set up an account using a fake name, and sometimes we just can't tell who the real person is behind a screen name—their online actions can have few consequences for them in the real world. Also, cyberbullies generally do not consider the consequences of their actions until after the fact, when it may be too late. Being bullied, online and in the real world, may lead the bullied person to depression and, in extreme cases, suicide. A research paper published in the *Journal of the American Medical Association Pediatrics* suggests cyberbullying and depression go hand in hand. Ten studies examined the link between social media victimization and depression, and all of them found a connection.[137]

The anonymity that gives rise to cyberbullying also promotes such unethical behaviors as trolling. Trolls are disruptive, often combative, and make offensive comments online without considering how their words may harm others. Trolling brings unhappiness because it is very difficult for the target to counteract the negative statements, and probably wise not to do so because it only encourages the behavior.

Research from Harvard University suggests that sharing information about ourselves on social media fires up the pleasure centers of our brain, which may explain the roots of social media addiction. Activities such as creating a personal blog, making a YouTube video, and loading pictures on Instagram all stimulate the pleasure center of our brain, which, according to the research, is positively associated with overall well-being, including life satisfaction and mental and physical heath.[138] If, as the research suggests, social media activities generally lead to an overall sense of well-being, the most likely explanation is because they enhance our psychological well-being: we feel better about ourselves and, at least with certain kinds of social networking activities, using social media can bring happiness and meaning to our lives.

Scientists believe that these feelings of wanting to share on social media trigger the release of dopamine in the brain. Dopamine increases attention, improves cognitive function, and stimulates creativity. It causes us to desire and seek pleasurable activities that enhance our well-being. Dopamine is stimulated by unpredictability, by gathering small bits of information, and by reward cues—pretty much the exact conditions social media presents. The pull of dopamine is so strong that studies have shown tweeting is harder for people to resist than cigarettes and alcohol. A short text or tweet (can be only 280 characters!) is a nugget of personal information to share that is ideally suited to sending our dopamine soaring.

Interestingly, a more recent Harvard study suggests that Facebook use, including liking others' posts, creating one's own posts, and clicking on links, is negatively associated with overall well-being. One possible explanation is that individuals believe that their own life compares poorly to what they see presented by others, even though this most likely results because other people tend to display only the most positive aspects of their life on social media.[139]

I also believe being happy is harder today than ever because of the negativity sometimes displayed on social media, the difficulty of gaining life satisfaction through social networking, and the decline of civility in society. We need to make a concerted effort to pursue happiness because of these constraints. Building lasting happiness is more challenging today. Someone might say something negative about us online or treat us uncivilly in the public arena and we're left feeling unsatisfied in our pursuit of happiness.

Whether or not we can gain happiness as a result of our

online behaviors, one thing is clear: we have less control over online relationships than we have over relationships in the real world we have chosen to develop into meaningful connections. Most of us know how actively engaging on social media sites can consume our time and attention. It can take us away from more important things, such as cultivating meaningful relationships in the real world. The artificial nature of online communications, where you can't see the other party, gauge body language, or just look into their eyes, can create a virtual world where the pursuit of happiness and meaning is linked to the behavior of others rather than to how we conduct our day-to-day affairs offline.

Years ago, these dynamics did not exist; today the face-to-face contact that used to be so prevalent is largely gone. It's easier to say and do uncivil things that make others unhappy when we're hiding behind an electronic device or dismissing others' feelings in discourse. So, achieving happiness today is more complicated, which is why learning the art of ethical behavior is so important.

How Does Meaning Fit into a Happy Life?

Meaning in life refers to whether our actions are worthwhile and are accompanied by a sense of value in our accomplishments.[140] Research in Positive Psychology suggests that happiness and meaning are, in fact, essential elements of well-being. Happiness and meaning are strongly correlated with each other, and often feed off each other. The more meaning we find in life, typically the happier we feel, and the happier we feel, the more we feel encouraged to pursue even greater meaning and purpose.[141]

Happiness can bring more meaning to our lives, but does not ensure it. Having an enjoyable first date can make us happy, but it is premature to say it adds meaning to our life. For that we'd need more time and experience to know how our partner contributes to our growth, self-worth, and sense of fulfillment, and us to theirs.

Similarly, greater meaning does not guarantee we will be happy. For example, a parent who consistently punishes a child for bad behavior may not feel happy about it but does feel a sense of having done the right thing (i.e., accomplished an important goal in life) by setting a good example and holding the child accountable.

Some research indicates that although happiness and meaning can be interrelated, they might not be all the time. In a paper published in the *Journal of Positive Psychology*, Roy Baumeister and a group of researchers from Stanford University surveyed 397 adults, looking for correlations among their levels of happiness, sense of meaning, and various other aspects of their lives, such as their behavior, moods, relationships, health, stress levels, work lives, and creative pursuits.

From their research, they learned that when people say they are happy it means they have positive emotions. When they say they are happy, they mean things are going well for them and they are satisfied with life. However, the time span of such happiness might not have been more than the length of a good day. Happiness, in this sense, is fleeting, and more of these happy events are needed to prolong happiness. Meaningful lives also generate positive emotions, and they deepen social connections, such as by allowing us to devote time to worthwhile causes, which increases our satisfaction with life and leads to more lasting happiness.[142]

There are those who say meaning in life is more important than happiness. Rabbi Harold Kushner, who wrote *When Bad Things Happen to Good People*, says: "You don't become happy by pursuing happiness. You become happy by living a life that means something." I agree with Rabbi Kushner up to a point: Living a meaningful life should lead to happiness because we set a goal, work toward it, and accomplish that goal. The goal gives us a purpose; the purpose gives us a direction; reaching the goal makes us feel like we have accomplished something important, and we feel happy having taken the journey and seen it through to its conclusion. But we shouldn't totally dismiss seeking happiness for happiness's sake, such as taking an enjoyable vacation after years of hard work.

What Contributes to Meaning in Life?

Baumeister, writing about issues related to self, self-esteem, and belongingness, suggests that questions about meaning are really about meaningfulness. *Meaningfulness* seems to entail a value judgment, or a cluster of them, which in turn implies a certain kind of emotion. When it comes to making life meaningful, people need to find value that casts their lives in a positive light, justifying who they are and what they do.[143]

Meaningfulness has a direct link to the ethical values discussed in Chapter 1. A meaningful life is one in which honesty rules over deception; kindness and compassion, not selfishness, are emphasized; and we are trustworthy and act responsibly toward others instead of trying to take advantage of them. Incorporating these values into everyday life can enhance our self-image, build self-esteem, enable growth and development, and lay the groundwork for self-actualization. Simply stated, it enables us to be all that we can be.

Emily Esfahani Smith writes in her book *The Power of*

Meaning that there are four pillars that help people find meaning in life. The following is a brief description of each pillar:[144]

1. *Belonging.* When we are understood, recognized, and approved of by those closest to us, it makes us feel like we belong to a community. Many people count their relationships as the most meaningful part of their lives, even when relationships are difficult or strained.

2. *Purpose.* When we have long-term goals in life that reflect our values and serve the greater good, we tend to think that our activities have more meaning.

3. *Storytelling.* When we understand relevant experiences in our life, we can begin to define who we are.

4. *Transcendence.* When we rise above, or transcend, our own needs, we can engage in behaviors that benefit others.

The essential point Smith makes is that by nurturing our relationships and serving others we can bring greater meaning to our lives. We should seek out activities that enable us to not only achieve happiness and meaning for ourselves but also enhance the well-being of others. It is through our actions and interactions that we gain meaning. We can also promote greater civility in society.

Reaching our full potential in life gives it meaning and allows us to feel fulfilled. The process is one of climbing to higher levels and at each stage satisfying higher-level needs. Before discussing the process, it's worth noting that Abraham Maslow's model of the hierarchy of needs (discussed next) has a cultural dimension that is based in Western values.

In Western culture, where individuality is highly valued, the notion of self-actualization arises from our understanding of the fact that individuals need to lead a self-fulfilling life, one that brings happiness and meaning. In contrast, in an Asian context, interpersonal relationships and social interactions and the group are valued more highly, on average, than self-actualization. In Eastern cultures, the need for self-actualization is replaced by needs for social status, admiration, and affiliation. In the East, autonomy and independence are not as important as, or at least have different connotations than, in the West.[145] The higher-level needs in an Asian context reflect the importance of respect, conformity to group/family needs, and standing in society. Happiness and meaning are achieved in the Asian context through collective good rather than individual accomplishment and self-expression, as in the Western world. Therefore, Maslow's hierarchy is built on a foundation of Western conceptualizations of happiness and meaning.

Maslow's Hierarchy of Needs

The *hierarchy of needs* is a motivational theory in psychology that is based on the work of psychologist Abraham Maslow from 1943 through 1970. Originally, the hierarchy consisted of a five-tier model of human needs, often depicted as ascending levels in a pyramid.[146] Maslow later revised his model, adding three more levels, so the hierarchy has eight tiers, as depicted in Figure 3.1.[147] Exhibit 3.3 provides some background on Maslow and his theory.

Figure 3.1
Maslow's Hierarchy of Needs Model

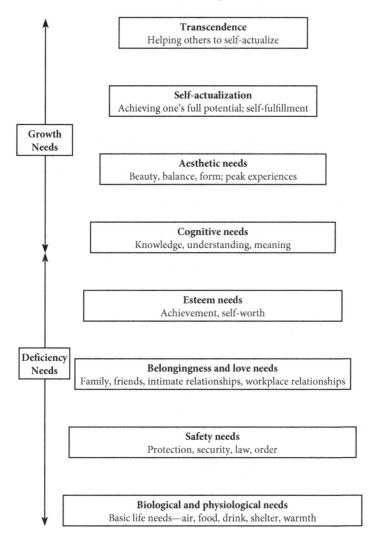

Exhibit 3.3

Abraham Maslow

Abraham Maslow (1908–1970) was a twentieth-century psychologist who developed a humanistic approach to psychology. He is best known for his hierarchy of needs. Maslow noted that some human needs were more powerful than others. He began to develop his theory in 1943 and distinguished five levels of human need, with each higher level building on the previous one. He continued to refine his theory and later proposed that the order may not be as rigid as he first thought.

Maslow believed that human motivation is based on people seeking fulfillment and change through personal growth. Self-actualized people are those who are fulfilled and doing all they are capable of. In studying eighteen people he considered self-actualized, including Abraham Lincoln, Albert Einstein, and Mahatma Gandhi, Maslow was able to identify fifteen characteristics of a self-actualized person, described below. These are related to growth needs engendered from fulfillment of potential and meaning in life or self-actualization. One characteristic of a self-actualized person is having strong moral/ethical standards.

According to Maslow, everything we do is derived from and revolves around a certain need we are seeking to satisfy. Initially, Maslow said that one must satisfy lower-level needs before moving on to meet higher-level growth needs. He later modified that claim, so some lower-level needs may not be fully met before we satisfy higher-level needs. For example, a person who lives in poverty, with a lack of food and shelter, can still develop loving relationships and build self-esteem.

Once our basic needs are met, we seek love and belonginess. These needs are met through creating satisfying relationships with family members and friends and positive workplace and online interactions. Developing meaningful relationships with others is important to building self-esteem because our relationships imply our acceptance by others.[148]

Self-esteem needs are met in close relationships that help us develop positive feelings of self-worth. These relationships can bring both happiness and greater meaning. Maslow classified esteem needs into two categories: (1) esteem for oneself (dignity, achievement, independence) and (2) reputation and respect from others (status, prestige).[149] Individuals at this level act to build pride in their work and themselves as people. Maslow suggested that people need both esteem from other people and inner self-respect before self-actualization is possible. If a person does not feel good about themselves and others don't value relationships with them, it seems a self-fulfilling life could not occur.

Moral virtues govern our behavior with others and build self-esteem; the more we use them in our relationships, the higher our self-esteem. Moderating our actions, maintaining self-control in relationships, and acting with courage enable self-esteem to flourish and bring happiness and meaning.

The first four levels of Maslow's hierarchy are essential for a person's well-being. Happiness results from satisfying relationships that build self-esteem, and meaningfulness results from a feeling of self-worth, recognition for one's work, and pride in accomplishments. Maslow refers to these as the deficiency needs. When these needs have been "more or less" satisfied, they go away, and our activities become directed toward higher growth needs, the upper four levels.[150]

Originally, self-actualization was the highest need in the hierarchy. *Self-actualization* is "loosely described as the full use and exploitation of talents, capabilities, potentialities, etc. Such people seem to be fulfilling themselves and to be doing the best that they are capable of doing. . . . They are people who have developed or are developing to the full stature of which they are capable."[151]

Maslow identified fifteen characteristics of self-actualizers:

1. They perceive reality efficiently and can tolerate uncertainty.

2. They accept themselves and others for who they are.

3. They are spontaneous in thought and action.

4. They are problem-centered, not self-centered.

5. They have an unusual sense of humor.

6. They are able to look at life objectively.

7. They are highly creative.

8. They are resistant to enculturation.

9. They are concerned for the welfare of humanity.

10. They are capable of deep appreciation of basic life experience.

11. They establish deep, satisfying relationships with a few people.

12. They have peak experiences.

13. They have a need for privacy.

14. They have democratic attitudes.

15. They have strong moral/ethical standards.

Although we could, theoretically, all achieve self-actualization, Maslow found only about 2 percent of the population reaches that state. This seems to be unexpectedly low and might be explained by the ascending levels in Maslow's initial model, which he backed off from as explained above. Still, he had developed the original model based on moving up one step at a time, so this may have established a bar that not many people could meet. In addition, he later proposed that the order in the hierarchy was not as rigid as he may have implied in his earlier description. For example, for some individuals the need for self-esteem might be more important than the need for love. For others, the need for creative fulfillment, part of the revised model described below, may supersede even the most basic needs.[152]

Beyond the flexibility in what was originally a rigid model, Maslow based his theories on the healthiest individuals from history. The average person might not fully possess the characteristics that would move them up to self-actualization so it could be said that, like the lower-level needs that don't have to be fully met, a self-actualized person might not meet the growth needs each and every time but by the preponderance of activities. It may be that the continuous pursuit of higher-level needs is most important to achieving self-actualization. In this way, we could liken it to developing virtues through practice and repetition in a variety of experiences. Hence, the 2 percent level may very well understate self-actualizers and we shouldn't be discouraged by it.

In the revised model, Maslow described two new levels between self-esteem and self-actualization. One is cognitive needs, including knowledge and meaning in life and understanding. These so-called self-awareness needs are similar to the intellectual virtues in Aristotle's virtue ethics: through knowledge and understanding of life's circumstances, an individual is better equipped to self-actualize and contribute to the betterment of others.

Maslow believed that humans have the need to increase their intelligence and thereby pursue knowledge in all its forms, including aesthetic ones. Aesthetic needs, the second level added above self-esteem, refer to appreciation of beauty, balance, and form, when things are creatively, beautifully, or artistically pleasing. Although he didn't address it specifically, we could say that aesthetic needs include an appreciation for the environment and sustainability.

In his later thinking, Maslow argued that there is a level of development beyond self-actualization, what he called *self-transcendence*. We achieve this level by focusing on things beyond the self, such as altruism, spiritual awakening, liberation from self-interested behavior, and the unity of being. Here is how he put it: "Transcendence refers to the very highest and most inclusive or holistic levels of human consciousness, behaving and relating, as ends rather than means, to oneself, to significant others, to human beings in general, to other species, to nature, and to the cosmos."[153]

Maslow suggested peak experiences can be thought of as transcendent moments that can be likened to spiritual experiences. These moments of ecstasy and complete happiness occur during artistic, athletic, or religious experiences. Moments in nature or intimate moments with family or friends provide these opportunities as well. Achieving an important goal, either a personal or collective one, could also lead to a peak experience. Other moments when such experiences might occur include when an individual helps another person in need or overcomes some type of adversity.[154]

Peak experiences are exceptional periods in life in which our talents are maximized. There is an expression in sports, "playing in the zone." These are peak experiences, when the athlete feels everything is going right and they transcend their usual limits of performance and go to a higher level.

Whereas *self-actualization* refers to fulfilling one's own potential, *transcendence* refers to attending to the needs of others. Transcendent experiences bring a clearer vision of the ideal, of what ought to be, of what actually could be, and therefore of what might be brought to pass.[155] We can think of transcendence as having concern for society—where it is headed and why—and, indeed, all the world.

Four characteristics of self-transcendence have been identified as follows:

1. Shift in focus: From the self to others, from selfishness and egoism to consideration of the needs of others.

2. Shift in values: From extrinsic motivation, or external rewards and demands, to intrinsic motivation (the reward for an activity is the activity itself).

3. Increase in moral concern: Self-transcendence occurs through a more intensive focus on doing what is right.

4. Emotions of elevation: Triggered by the three above, these emotions include awe, ecstasy, amazement, feeling uplifted, feeling elevated.[156]

These characteristics are consistent with virtuous behavior and are an integral part of human flourishing.

The upper four levels of the hierarchy constitute a person's growth needs. These can never be satisfied completely. Unlike the deficiency needs, for which satisfying them lessens the need, the individual's motivation to pursue growth needs only increases. The more they are satisfied, the more people pursue them. For example, the more one comes to understand, the more one becomes motivated to learn and grow.[157] So, the pursuit of growth needs is an ongoing experience and may account for why Maslow found such a low level of self-actualization.

Maslow's classifications provide insight into how we can achieve greater meaning in our life through virtuous behavior. First, there is the importance of knowledge and understanding as cognitive needs, which elevates intellectual virtues as providing a thought process to achieve greater meaning. Second, Maslow recognized the importance of strong moral/ethical standards, which implies a person may not reach the level of self-actualization without being able to distinguish between good and bad, right and wrong, and acting on those beliefs. Third, integrity is essential to reaching the highest levels that transcend self-awareness and attend to the interests of others. Last, through transcendence contributing to the betterment of society provides a link to civic duty and increasing civility in society.

What Prevents a Meaningful Life?

If you have a selfish streak in you, then you'll focus on satisfying your own needs regardless of how that affects others. Meaningful relationships depend on a give-and-take. You should do kind things for others, be understanding of their needs, and act in their best interests without sacrificing your own happiness. Seek respect, not attention.

Be understanding of yourself. You may make mistakes, not accomplish what you want, be criticized for your actions, so use these occasions to grow as a person, develop greater patience, redefine your goals if necessary, and look at the bigger picture: How can you contribute to the betterment of society?

Meaningfulness also comes from being open to new things: new relationships, new challenges. Step out of your comfort zone from time to time to create just enough stress to enhance your ability to focus, be creative, achieve more than you feel capable of, and deal with unexpected events with a more measured response.[158]

Forcing yourself into discomfort and then seeing the result keeps you pushing yourself. When there's an element of uncertainty that you learn to deal with, your confidence level increases and you're better prepared to accept new challenges that can promote self-actualization.

What if we're not ethical people? Can we achieve a meaningful life? It wouldn't seem so because we may be ambivalent toward others, focus on our own needs without regard to how that affects others, or simply ignore our moral duties as members of humanity. It's hard to imagine developing meaningful relationships and self-actualizing behavior without a strong sense of right and wrong.

What if we are unmotivated at work, look for the easy way out, and fail to meet our work obligations on a consistent basis? It would seem unlikely that we could reach our full potential and be self-fulfilled. Although people do not have to rise to the top in an organization to build self-esteem, it does seem that pursuing excellence advances happiness and greater meaning in life.

Life is full of challenging situations, and the way we deal with them can affect meaningfulness. If we successfully navigate the ups and downs and achieve our goals, then we should feel competent in what we have done, a sense of accomplishment, and greater self-confidence. However, conflicts between our interests and those of others that go unresolved can make it more difficult to achieve meaningfulness. Our cognitive abilities enable us to understand what causes the conflict and how we can resolve it through ethical reasoning by meeting our obligations to others.

Kant argued that the good will freely chooses to do its moral duty. That duty, in turn, is motivated solely by reason. Because the dictates of reason allow for no exceptions, moral duty is absolute. To have a good will means to be motivated to do the right thing out of a sense of moral duty. Doing the right thing adds meaning to our lives because it provides an inner sense of having treated others humanely, not having used them for our own desires, and respecting them and allowing them the freedom to act as they will.

Do we have a moral duty to seek the highest levels of Maslow's hierarchy? Yes, because by achieving our full potential we are better able to add meaningfulness to the life of others by attending to their needs through transcendent experiences.

Conclusion

The successful pursuit of happiness and meaning requires a commitment to ethical behavior. It depends on our willingness to call upon what is good in ourselves to achieve our highest needs and deal with conflicts that may arise along the way. We can reach a state of self-actualization if we apply our ethical reasoning skills to gain knowledge and understanding of life's circumstances, exercise self-control when choices exist, demonstrate moral courage to deal with ethical challenges, and look beyond ourselves to improve the lives of others.

Ethics does not occur in a vacuum. We can use the ethical skills discussed in this book and bring them to bear in life's circumstances. We can reach out to others and improve their lives, which, in turn, adds meaning to our lives. We can achieve transcendent experiences and grow as individuals. We can bring those abilities into the workplace and enhance ethics in organizations. More will be said about that in the next chapter.

CHAPTER 4

Applied Ethics

Our business success is directly linked to enhancing the well-being of the people who make and enjoy our products and to supporting the communities where we grow our ingredients.

—Irene Rosenfield, former CEO and chair of the board of directors of Mondelez International, an American multinational food and beverage company

Notice how the statement recognizes an obligation to enhance the well-being of the stakeholders. *Stakeholders* include the parties affected by decisions and, in a business sense, include customers/clients, employees, top management, the business entity, government, the community, and the decision maker.

Companies have an ethical obligation to serve the best interests of society, but in reality, some have focused on their own self-interests to the detriment of society. Just as pursuing self-interests, using an *end justifies the means* philosophy and rationalizing unethical behavior can make it more difficult for individuals to act ethically, the same could be said about a business, nonprofit, or any other entity. These entities should apply ethical reasoning much like an individual does to evaluate how their decisions might affect the well-being of stakeholders.

Analyzing harms and benefits, moral duties, and virtue is just as important for entities as for individuals. The cases chosen for discussion in this chapter have one common theme: putting profits over people. You'll learn about well-known companies that made controversial decisions that impacted society in a substantial way, why they made those decisions, and the role of ethics in their decision-making process. These are cautionary tales in which you can see the implications of faulty ethical reasoning and how it played out in the real world. You'll also learn about individuals who faced ethical dilemmas and how they balanced self-interest with doing what is right.

What Is Applied Ethics?

Applied ethics is a branch of ethics that deals with the practical application of ethical considerations to moral problems, practices, and policies in the areas of private/personal life, social networking activities, technology, professional practice, health and science, the environment, and business. Normative ethical theories are used for the analysis, examining whether the decisions were right or wrong, good or bad. Try to apply your knowledge of ethics in each situation. As we analyze each dilemma, put yourself in the position of the decision makers and consider what you might have done differently in light of how the intended action affected the well-being of stakeholders.

Ethics in Business

The principles of business ethics are no different from the principles of ethical behavior in our personal lives. Just as individuals should consider whether their choices treat others the way they would wish to be treated, so should businesses. Just as each of us is affected by business decisions, so, too, are businesses affected by the actions of other businesses. The ethical values that underlie business decisions are similar to those we face in everyday life. Businesses need to deal honestly with stakeholders, be trustworthy, understand the needs of stakeholders (i.e., be empathetic), and accept responsibility for their actions.

Businesses should also act in accordance with virtues such as by exercising self-control, showing moral courage, and acting justly. Exercising self-control means not making decisions that completely ignore the interests of stakeholders or overcompensating for their needs but rather pursuing the legitimate right of business to earn a profit. Moral courage is important because those in the know about corporate wrongdoing—whistleblowers—should feel comfortable using the internal reporting process so they don't have to take the extreme act of blowing the whistle in public or ignoring the situation. Businesses have an ethical obligation to provide an outlet for would-be whistleblowers to use internal means and not retaliate against them. Just decisions are those that treat the stakeholders fairly, without bias toward the needs of one group or another unless there is a reasonable basis to do so. For example, two suppliers that submit bids to provide product should be treated the same unless one has a lower-cost or higher-quality product or better service.

One reason businesses still struggle with ethical behavior is they are not aware of their role as moral agents. A *moral agent* is a person (or entity) who has the ability to distinguish between right and wrong and is accountable for their actions. Moral agents have a moral responsibility not to cause unjust harm. Individuals in business play a moral agency role because their decisions affect the well-being of others. The idea that a business has moral agency obligations stems in part from U.S. Supreme Court decisions declaring that a corporation is a person in the eyes of the law—at least for some purposes. For example, corporations have a right to have their contracts respected by the government. Shareholders/owners generally cannot be sued. Instead, the corporate entity could be sued if its actions are similar to those of an individual who broke the law or violates ethical norms.

In a popular opinion piece published in the September 1970 edition of the *New York Times Magazine*, Milton Friedman, an economist who is well known for capitalist philosophy, offered the following quote: "There is one and only one social responsibility of business—to increase its profits." This quote has been taken out of context because it omits the rest of the statement, which is "to use its resources and engage in activities designed to increase its profits so long as it stays within the rules of the game, which is to say, engages in open and free competition without deception or fraud." In the latter part of the statement, Friedman meant that businesses should not commit fraud on customers, employees, suppliers, shareholders, and other stakeholders whose interests would be harmed by such actions in the pursuit of profit.[159] That is their moral obligation.

Adam Smith (1723–1790) is known as the father of modern capitalism. His major work, *An Inquiry into the Nature and Causes of the Wealth of Nations* (1776), outlines the basis for free-market capitalism. Laissez-faire philosophies in capitalism, such as minimizing the role of government intervention and taxation in the free markets, and the idea that an "invisible hand" guides supply and demand, are key elements of his political philosophy. His famous statement that expresses that philosophy is: "It's not from the benevolence of the butcher, the brewer, or the baker, that we can expect our dinner, but from their regard to their own interest."[160] Smith meant that each person, by looking out for his or her self-interest, inadvertently helps to create the best outcome for all.

At first glance it may seem that Smith was a proponent of egoistic corporate behavior, and maybe he was. But it wasn't without limitations. Even before Smith wrote *The Wealth of Nations*, he produced a treatise on moral philosophy. *The Theory of Moral Sentiments* (1759) makes the case that business should be guided by the morals of good people. Smith sets forth a theory of how we come to be moral, of how morality functions on both individual and societal levels, and what forces are likely to corrupt our sense of morality, which is derived from our capacity to sympathize directly and indirectly with other people. This occurs by feeling what others actually feel in their circumstances. He believed we could achieve this moral perspective because of our conscience, which allows us to envision our own actions just as a disinterested observer might.[161] Thus, Smith's philosophy was more akin to enlightened egoism in that the interests of others should be considered (sympathized with) in making moral decisions.

How do we do so? According to Smith, by recognizing the importance of virtuous behavior by adopting dispositions such as kindness, empathy, patience, endurance, and courage.[162]

Establishing an Ethical Culture

Corporate culture is the shared beliefs of top managers in a company about how they should manage themselves and other employees and how they should conduct their business. Corporate culture starts with an explicit statement of values, beliefs, and customs from top management that guide ethical decision making.

An important element of ethical culture is the tone at the top. *Tone at the top* refers to the ethical environment that is created in the workplace by the organization's leadership. An ethical tone creates the basis for standards of behavior that become part of the code of ethics.[163] Setting an ethical tone is a necessary but insufficient basis to expect ethical behavior to occur in a business. The actions of top managers must match the tone to have that effect. In other words, top managers must "walk the talk" of ethics. For example, if top management only pays lip service to claims of a hostile work environment, actions such as sexual harassment may not be taken seriously and abusive behaviors may continue unabated.

The tone set by managers influences how employees respond to ethical challenges and is enhanced by ethical leadership. When leaders are perceived as trustworthy, employee trust increases; leaders are seen as ethical and as honoring a higher level of duties.[164]

If the tone set by management upholds ethics and integrity, employees will be more inclined to uphold those same values. However, if top management appears unconcerned about ethics and focuses solely on profitability, employees will be more prone to accept improper behavior by managers, such as fraud, and may engage in it themselves. *Fraud* is a willful act that violates the law with the intention of deceiving another party. The Wells Fargo case discussed later is one such example.

Applying the foregoing concepts to ethical decision making enables us to better understand the motivating factors of the unethical behavior in the following cases studies and how and why stakeholder needs were left out of the mix. I selected these cases because, for the most part, they are well known and illustrate in a dramatic way how self-serving decisions in business can affect the well-being of the rest of us.

The Ford Pinto: The Dangers of Using Cost–Benefit Analysis

The Pinto was Ford Motor Company's first domestic North American subcompact automobile, marketed beginning on September 11, 1970. Shortly thereafter, the public was shocked to find out that if the Pinto experienced an impact at speeds of only thirty miles per hour or lower, they could become engulfed in flames and passengers could be burned or even die. Ford faced an ethical dilemma: what to do about the apparently unsafe gas tanks that seemed to be the cause of these incidents. Back then, the gas tanks were in the rear behind the license plate, so a rear-end collision might cause the fire. Ford's initial reaction was to dismiss the problem, stating it had followed all the safety laws in effect and the placement of its gas tank was comparable to that in other compact cars. That was true. The company invoked the rationalization that if something is legal, it is, therefore, ethical. Hence, Ford was willing to accept that it had an unsafe product because it hadn't violated any laws.

A risk–benefit analysis tool was available to assist Ford in its decision making. The National Highway Traffic Safety Administration (NHTSA) developed this tool, which excused a defendant from being penalized if the monetary costs of making a production change were greater than the "societal benefit" of that change. The analysis followed the same approach modeled in Judge Learned Hand's ruling in *United States v. Carroll*

Towing in 1947, which boiled down the theory of negligence to the following: If the expected harm exceeded the cost to prevent it, the defendant was obligated to take the precaution, and if they did not, liability would result. But if the cost was larger than the expected harm, the defendant was not expected to take the precaution. If there was an accident, the defendant would not be found guilty.[165]

The ethical question for Ford was whether a risk–benefit analysis should be used in a situation where a defect in design or manufacturing could lead to death or serious bodily harm.[166] Ford suffered from ethical blind spots in that it failed to see that relying on the outcome of a risk–benefit analysis could mask the overall moral duty of an automobile company to ensure its cars are safe and protective of life. Ford put profits, or at least cost minimization, ahead of the safety of the driving public, as explained next.

Ford did do a risk–benefit analysis to decide on an appropriate course of action using the following data.[167]

Ford's Risk–Benefit Analysis

Benefits of fixing the Pinto:

1. *Savings:* 180 burn deaths, 180 serious burn injuries, 2,100 burned vehicles

2. *Unit cost:* $200,000 per death (figure provided by the government); $67,000 per burn injury, and $700 to repair a burned vehicle (company estimates)

3. *Total benefits:* 180 × ($200,000) + 180 × ($67,000) + 2,100 × ($700) = **$49.5 million**

Costs of fixing the Pinto:

1. *Sales:* 11 million cars, 1.5 million light trucks
2. *Unit cost:* $11 per car, $11 per light truck
3. *Total cost:* 11,000,000 × ($11) + 1,500,000 × ($11) = **$137 million**

On the basis of this analysis, Ford decided not to change the placement of the fuel tank. It would appear Ford and other car companies learned their lesson after the incident described below and added two safety features: rear-end bumpers and gas tanks moved to the side of the car.

Ford's risk–benefit analysis relied on utilitarian reasoning, an approach that reduces a decision to dollar considerations. One problem with the analysis is there was no way to know the extent of lawsuits brought by the driving public and what they might cost Ford. For example, in May 1972, Lily Gray was traveling with thirteen-year-old Richard Grimshaw when their Pinto was struck by another car traveling approximately thirty miles per hour. The impact ignited a fire in the Pinto, which killed Lily Gray and left Grimshaw with devastating injuries. A judgment was rendered against Ford, and the jury awarded the Gray family $560,000 and Matthew Grimshaw, the father of Richard Grimshaw, $2.5 million in compensatory damages. The surprise came when the jury also awarded $125 million in punitive damages. This was subsequently reduced to $3.5 million.[168]

A bigger flaw in Ford's reasoning was its blindness to the rights of the driving public. The question Ford should have addressed is: Doesn't the driving public have a right to get into their cars and not expect them to explode from rear-end collisions?

Ford also didn't seem to understand its social responsibilities that imposed an ethical obligation to serve the best interests of stakeholders and advance the cause of ethics in society. The public lost trust in Ford, and by 1980 the company stopped making the Pinto.

Ford would have benefited by checking itself before making a final decision: Knowing what they knew, how would Ford managers have felt if a loved one drove a Pinto? Would they have changed their decision? Perhaps not, but looking at it from another's perspective could have helped decision makers focus on what's most important—the safety of the driving public.

As with all of the cases discussed below, Ford knew about the safety problem but chose to ignore it. Why? Its decision was influenced by the high cost to fix the cars and the dismissal of safety concerns. Its faulty reasoning illustrates the dangers of using a harms versus benefits analysis. Utilitarianism is a useful method of ethical reasoning, but it's not foolproof, as the Pinto case clearly illustrates.

Ford would have been better served by following the deontology philosophy that calls for treating others as members of humanity and taking actions that would be considered universally acceptable. In other words, Ford had a duty to provide the safest car possible because, if it had thought about the situation ethically, that is the way Ford should have wanted all car manufacturers to act. Just imagine if each one had a different safety issue that threatened the security of the driving public. We can also think about Maslow's hierarchy of needs that includes safety as a deficiency need. How could a car company dismiss such a basic need?

Driving our cars is supposed to be a pleasant experience, but how can it be when safety concerns exist? Our happiness comes from many forms of activity and driving our cars is one of them. The Pinto case illustrates how the well-being of the public can be disregarded when profit considerations take the fore.

It's interesting to consider whether any of the Ford executives who were involved in the decision-making process would have predicted in advance that they would have made such an unethical choice. Dennis Gioia, who was in charge of recalling defective automobiles at Ford, did not advocate ordering a recall. Gioia eventually came to view his decision not to recall the Pinto as a moral failure.

Takata Airbags: Putting Profits over Human Lives

On July 16, 2018, Ford Motor Company agreed to a so-called economic loss settlement of $299.1 million, covering at least 6 million U.S. vehicles with potentially faulty Takata airbag inflators. The settlement covers claims that vehicles were inaccurately represented to be safe and that buyers had overpaid for cars with defective or substandard airbags. The settlements cover out-of-pocket costs, including lost wages and child care costs Ford owners may face, or already incurred, to get vehicles repaired. Ford's class action settlement agreement over Takata airbags affects 37 million vehicles and 50 million airbags.[169] Six automakers had previously agreed to similar settlements worth over $1.2 billion combined.

At least twenty-four deaths worldwide have been linked to the rupturing of faulty Takata airbag inflators as of April 2019. More than 290 injuries worldwide are also linked to Takata inflators that can explode, releasing metal shrapnel inside cars and trucks. The airbags can explode because the ammonium nitrate in them can become unstable over time, especially after exposure to temperature fluctuations and periods of constant high humidity. This can lead to inflators exploding with unexpectedly violent force and spraying metal shrapnel. Drivers and passengers in the United States have died from blunt force trauma, from injuries to the head and neck, and from massive bleeding from lacerations caused by the flying metal.

Did the automakers know about the problem with the Takata airbags? The legal filing by the plaintiffs says emails and internal documents turned over by Honda show that in 1999 and 2000, the automaker was intimately involved in developing a problematic propellant, or explosive, used in Takata airbags. The propellant raised concerns internally at Takata because at least two inflators ruptured, according to the filing. Still, Honda pushed for the Takata airbags despite the quality issues because they were relatively inexpensive.[170]

Ford chose Takata's inflators over the objections of the automaker's own inflator expert, who opposed the use of Takata's propellant because of its instability and sensitivity to moisture. Ford overrode those objections because it thought Takata was the only supplier that could provide the large number of inflators it needed.

So, here again we have car companies that put cost considerations over safety of the public. Knowingly ignoring safety concerns that have been raised by company experts to avoid cost issues is a clear-cut example of corporate greed. Egoism drove the decisions of the automakers as they looked out for their own interests and ignored the safety concerns of the public.

Had the car companies used an enlightened egoism perspective, they would have at least considered how their intended actions could affect the driving public with respect to safety concerns, possible legal actions after accidents, and so on. That doesn't mean the decision would have been different. The only way for that to have happened would have been for the car companies to adhere to the same moral duty that Ford faced in the Pinto case: "Never sacrifice the safety of the driving public for cost considerations."

Volkswagen Carbon Emissions Defeat Device

On September 18, 2015, the U.S. Environmental Protection Agency (EPA) reported that Volkswagen (VW) had installed so-called defeat devices in hundreds of thousands of 2.0-liter engines in the United States since 2009. The devices were installed in VWs, Porsches, and Audis to help the cars meet exhaust pollution standards when monitored in tests even when their emissions levels actually exceeded the limits.

Four days later, the company admitted that some 11 million diesel vehicles worldwide, including 8.5 million in Europe and 600,000 in the United States, had been fitted with software that enabled them to report lower levels of carbon pollutants than really existed, thereby sacrificing the health of the driving public and raising environmental concerns. Investigators found that some cars emitted up to forty times more harmful nitrogen oxide—linked to respiratory and cardiovascular diseases—than legally allowed. As recently as May 2018, Germany ordered Porsche and Audi each to recall 60,000 vehicles across Europe that were found with the software. Other facts of the case are as follows:[171]

- VW chief executive Martin Winterkorn resigned after the scandal broke. On May 3, 2018, he was charged with alleged conspiracy to defraud the United States and VW customers.

- VW pleaded guilty to a U.S. criminal case in March 2017, settling its legal entanglements by adding $4.4 billion in criminal and civil fines to $17.5 billion it had already agreed to pay in compensation to owners of 580,000 tainted diesels sold in the United States through a buyback program, lease termination, or modification of the affected 2.0-liter vehicles.

- VW agreed to spend $4.7 billion to mitigate pollutions and make investments that support zero-emission vehicle technology.

- The settlements in the United States also resolved claims by the Federal Trade Commission that VW violated the law through deceptive and unfair advertising and sale of its "clean diesel" vehicles.

- VW agreed to pay a fine of 1 billion euros (about $860 million) to settle a probe by German prosecutors.

- On September 10, 2018, shareholders of Volkswagen representing 1,670 claims filed a lawsuit against the company for $10.7 billion in damages over the scandal, which has already cost VW $23.6 billion.

A statement of facts published as part of a settlement with the U.S. Department of Justice admitted that VW engineers struggled to make a diesel engine that would both perform well and be capable of meeting stringent U.S. emissions standards. It explained how instead they designed a system to switch on emissions controls when the cars were being tested, and then turn them off during normal driving. It also described how managers repeatedly sanctioned the use of the system, despite objections from some employees, and encouraged engineers to cover up what they were doing.[172]

How could a company be so blind to the ethical issues as to risk the well-being of the public in the name of profits? It's not as if VW top managers didn't know about the defeat devices. A study by the International Council on Clean Transport showed that VW diesels were producing far higher emissions on the road than in official lab tests. Senior managers were warned, yet did nothing about it. The ethical fault in VW's decision-making process was to adopt the idea that the end justifies the means. The end goal was to sell a car that would pass emissions inspections in the United States and cost less to manufacture, while the means was to install a defeat device. VW sacrificed the health and welfare of the driving public in the name of profits. We might ask: Imagine if every car company did something like VW. Health and safety concerns would skyrocket. Damage to the environment might be alarming.

Oliver Schmidt, former general manager of VW's Engineering and Environmental Office, was part of a group of engineers who engaged in the illegal activity ostensibly because they were afraid to admit to feared top executives that they couldn't reconcile the company's goals and the law's demands. Fear of top management establishes a culture that blocks ethical actions when top management itself promotes unethical behavior. Responsible behavior gave way to corporate malfeasance.

On September 6, 2017, Schmidt pleaded guilty to conspiracy to defraud the U.S. government and to violating the Clean Air Act. He was fined $400,000.

In announcing the legal ruling on Schmidt, Judge Sean Cox stated: "His punishment was designed to further 'general deterrence,'" explaining that "the point was to send a message to other corporate officials that following illegal orders is not defense." Cox also told Schmidt, somewhat apologetically, that "his job requires him to imprison 'good people just making very, very bad decisions.'"[173]

"Just following orders" is not a defense for going along with unethical decisions made at the highest level of a company.

The Betty Vinson case discussed in Chapter 2 offers a similar explanation for why an employee did not speak out and do something to stop fraud. Fear of the potential repercussions of speaking out is a strong motivator for silence. This is why corporate culture should encourage speaking out to protect the interests of the public, which expects corporations to act in an ethical manner.

The judge's statement that Schmidt was a good person doing bad things illustrates how a person can get caught up in illegal or unethical actions even though they "normally" wouldn't do such things. Thus, there can be a cognitive gap between a person's view of themselves as a good person and what they do that cannot be called good.

Wells Fargo: Profits over Customer Service

Back in 2016 it was disclosed that Wells Fargo Bank had scammed customers out of millions of dollars by setting up unauthorized accounts as part of an incentive compensation plan. Bank employees were pressured into selling unwanted products and even setting up accounts in customers' names that were not requested. For example, if a customer opened a checking account, the bank would encourage them to accept a credit card or take out an automobile loan, a practice known as cross-selling. If the customer didn't, they still might have found themselves receiving a credit card in the mail. The following facts illustrate the extent of improper actions taken by Wells Fargo:[174]

Improper Practices

- Opened 3.5 million fake bank and credit card accounts in customers' names.

- Improperly charged mortgage fees known as rate-lock extensions when loan approvals exceeded the 30- to 45-day period. These fees were charged even though the delay in approvals were caused by the bank, not the customer.

- Set up about 528,000 unauthorized online bill-paying services.

- Forced up to 800,000 borrowers into unneeded auto insurance for collisions. The cost of unneeded insurance pushed about 274,000 Wells Fargo customers into delinquency and caused nearly 25,000 wrongful vehicle repossessions.

- Mortgage division changed loan terms, falsified records, and even stole money from mortgage bond investors.

Fines and Penalties

- Paid $1.2 billion to the U.S. government for hiding bad mortgage loans from its government-guaranteed loan program in years leading up to the home mortgage crash.

- Paid $142 million in fines for the fraud under a national class action lawsuit.

- Paid an additional $480 million to settle lawsuits brought by shareholders.

- Separately, agreed to pay $575 million to states related to cross-selling practices.

- Refunded $3.7 million in bank account fees charged on unauthorized accounts and lines of credit.

- Paid an additional $5.4 million for illegal vehicle sei-
  zures for repossessing more than 860 vehicles of U.S.
  service members in violation of the Servicemembers
  Civil Relief Act.

As a result of the massive fraud, the bank terminated 5,300
employees and managers, about 1 percent of its workforce. To
add fuel to the fire, the bank fired whistleblowers who tried to
warn the bank of the improper practices.

Why did all this happen? One reason was bank profits took
a hit during the financial recession in 2007–2008. Beyond that,
the cause of the massive fraud was the way in which the bank
was run, or its corporate governance systems, as evidenced by
following:

Corporate Governance Failures

- Unethical tone at the top: top management sanctioned the improper practices. The attitude was, Do
  as I say; be a team player.
- Toxic corporate culture that emphasized profits over
  customer service.
- Conflict of interests between incentive compensation
  plan and serving customer interests. Employees
  needed to break the rules to maximize their incentive
  compensation.
- Fiduciary obligation to watch over customer needs
  and protect their funds was violated; customers were
  not treated fairly.
- Failure of ethical leadership.
- Former CEO, John Stumpf, resigned shortly after the
  scandal broke amid severe criticism by Congress in

its Senate Banking Committee hearing on the fraud on September 20, 2016.

Wells Fargo violated the trust of its customers, acted irresponsibly, and set up a system of incentive compensation that created an environment that convinced employees that the ends of maximizing their compensation justified the means of establishing fake accounts and cross-selling products and services. Though the bank may not have knowingly followed a utilitarian analysis to determine what it would do, as did Ford in the Pinto case, its actions illustrate the danger of putting the ends ahead of the means. The bank overvalued its own interests and, presumably, the interests of employees who would receive incentive compensation (ends), while undervaluing customer service and selling unwanted products (means).

How could so many employees and managers go along with the fraud? The workers who were fired for gaming the system said they were just following orders in the sense that the bank pressured them to engage in these wrongful practices to increase bank profits. Some tried to blow the whistle on wrongdoing but were fired for trying to do the right thing. One such person was Jessie Guitron, a former employee of Wells Fargo, who warned the bank of the improper practices, stating in an interview with CBS News that she complained over and over again to no avail. She said: "I was doing what my conscience was telling me to do. It's fraud. That's what it is."[175]

The bank's failures had negative effects on the well-being of affected customers, who paid extra fees for unwanted services and products. Some had their autos repossessed or were forced into delinquency on their loans.

Wells Fargo is an example of how a corporation can

take advantage of customers in the name of profits without thinking twice about what it is doing and why. It would be an understatement to say the bank had ethical blind spots. More accurately, it lacked a moral conscience.

We are not masters of our own destiny when our day-to-day experiences can be tainted by the actions of corporate entities.

McDonald's Hot Coffee

Personal responsibility is an important aspect of ethical behavior. A classic case in which a person's own actions might have caused harm is the McDonald's hot coffee case. It illustrates that we need to exercise care in using products when a safety component is present. Perhaps we can't (shouldn't) blame companies when our own negligence contributes to the problem.

In 1992, seventy-nine-year-old Stella Liebeck bought a cup of takeout coffee at a McDonald's drive-through and spilled the entire contents on her lap when the cup tipped over when she opened the lid to add cream and sugar. The car was not moving at the time, but Liebeck did have the cup between her knees. The spill caused third-degree burns (the most serious kind) and required skin grafts on her inner thighs and elsewhere.[176] Liebeck brought a lawsuit against McDonald's claiming the coffee was "defective" because it was sold at a higher temperature than safe—190 degrees Fahrenheit, near boiling point, and 20 degrees more than is generally considered safe.

The following facts were revealed in the case:[177]

- McDonald's admitted it knew about the risk of serious burns from its scalding-hot coffee for more than ten years. The risk was repeatedly brought to its attention through numerous other claims and lawsuits, including reports from seven hundred people who burned themselves.

- An expert witness for the company testified that the number of burns was insignificant compared to the billions of cups of coffee the company served each year.

- McDonald's quality assurance manager testified that the coffee, at the temperature it was poured into Styrofoam cups, was not fit for human consumption because it would burn the mouth and throat.

- The company admitted the consumers were unaware of the extent of the risk of serious burns from spilled coffee served at the 190 degree temperature. It did not warn customers and offered no explanation why.

Liebeck didn't want to go to court, but after she asked for $20,000 for medical expenses and McDonald's offered to pay only $800, she decided to file a lawsuit. After hearing the evidence, the jury concluded that McDonald's handling of its coffee was so irresponsible that Liebeck should get much more and awarded her $200,000 for compensatory damages, which was later reduced to $160,000 after determining that 20 percent of the fault lay with Liebeck for spilling the coffee. The jury then found McDonald's had engaged in willful, reckless, malicious conduct and awarded $2.7 million in punitive damages, which was ultimately reduced to $480,000. McDonald's has changed how it heats up its coffee.

This is a case that raised the issue about frivolous (time-wasting) lawsuits. Many felt Liebeck was to blame because no one should place a cup of hot coffee between their knees, open it up, and add to the contents. It was her fault, she was reckless, she should have known better simply because coffee is hot. Others said that McDonald's was to blame because it had received previous complaints and knew the coffee was sold above industry standards for temperature. Why didn't McDonald's simply lower the temperature once it was clear there was a problem? Perhaps because there is a perception that hot coffee means fresher coffee and many people put cold cream in the coffee to cool it down.

McDonald's ethical reasoning was much like Ford's with the Pinto. The number of burns from the hot coffee was insignificant compared with the number of cups sold, so lowering the temperature made no sense from a cost–benefit analysis, just as fixing the gas tank would cost much more than letting the cost of injuries play out.

In light of the Pinto case, Takata airbags, Wells Fargo, and McDonald's, it would be refreshing to see companies apply a rule utilitarian reasoning approach and evaluate their intended actions against rules such as "never sell a product to the public that may cause harm." It would also be a welcome change if they listened to whistleblowers who warn of possible pain and suffering to the public. Pain and suffering bring unhappiness and make it virtually impossible to enjoy using the products.

It's troubling that time and again we hear of companies that dismiss possible problems with the safety of their products in the name of cost–benefit analysis. What's missing is the reality check that companies have a moral duty to consider how a product might affect the well-being of customers. Perhaps this is because some people believe there is (or should be) a different standard for personal ethics than for business ethics, implying the latter has a lesser standard. This doesn't make ethical sense because the makers of products are individuals, and corporations are treated as persons in the eyes of the law.

How Decisions Can Affect Well-Being

Turning now to how decisions made by individuals can affect well-being, we'll examine three cases with the following themes:

Case	Theme
Bernie Madoff	Using one's position to gain trust and scam investors
Jeffrey Wigand	Blowing the whistle without regard to personal costs
Edward Snowden	Putting the public interest over self-interest while ignoring the law

Bernie Madoff: A Scammer Extraordinaire

Bernie Madoff was a successful financier who became wealthy by promising investors high returns using a Ponzi scheme. A *Ponzi scheme* is a fraudulent investing scam that promises high rates of return with little risk to investors. The Ponzi scheme generates returns for older investors by acquiring new investors and using their investment dollars to pay returns rather than earning returns through legitimate investments.[178]

Madoff used much of the invested funds for personal purposes and was able to perpetuate the scheme because there was no shortage of investors in the early 2000s, when the stock market was booming. However, when boom turned to bust during the recession, and investors asked for their money back, Madoff was unable to comply, having spent much of the money on himself and family. By the time the dust settled, Madoff had perpetrated a $65 billion fraud. He was sentenced to 150 years in prison for running the biggest fraudulent scheme in U.S. history.

Madoff's story is one of misplaced trust. Investors knew him personally, respected all that he had accomplished, and never thought they would be betrayed. After all, Madoff was the chairman of the Nasdaq Stock Market, the second largest market in the United States after the New York Stock Exchange. He was a benefactor in the community and friend to many. Madoff was held in high esteem by the investing public and that enabled him to pull off the Ponzi scheme.

More than 2,200 people had invested roughly $20 billion with Madoff. His client list included the likes of Hollywood director Steven Spielberg, real estate magnate Mortimer Zuckerman, actor Kevin Bacon, and Hall of Fame pitcher Sandy Koufax. Madoff's scamming hurt many, and it's safe to say their happiness was compromised by Madoff's actions.

Madoff told investors that the investments had grown to $65 billion. Lawyers charged with recovering as much money as possible to make investors whole have been able to come up with about $13.3 billion, as of December 8, 2018. This is about 70 percent of the $20 billion that he took from investors. The $45 billion differential was the nonexistent returns on investments. Given the recoveries so far, it may sound like the investors weren't harmed as badly as they could have been. But their $20 billion investments might have doubled in value had the money been legitimately invested.

In an unintended consequence, the investors had to pay federal capital gains tax on the (falsely) reported increase of $45 billion in investment income that never existed. The federal government is allowing investors, who have collectively paid billions in taxes on money they never really had, to take twenty years of federal tax credits as reimbursement for some of the overpayments, but it will not refund their money.[179] Given that most of Madoff's investors were retired people, they may never see the benefit of the tax credits.

We can get a glimpse into what Madoff was thinking when he decided to scam so many investors in his responses to a phone interview with professor Eugene Soltes. Madoff said:

> In hindsight, when I look back, it wasn't as if I couldn't have said no. . . . It wasn't like I was being blackmailed into doing something, or that I was afraid of getting caught doing it. . . . I sort of rationalized that what I was doing was OK, that it wasn't going to hurt anybody.

Madoff also said he had built his confidence to a level where he felt there was nothing that he couldn't attain.[180]

We might characterize Madoff's behavior as narcissistic. According to Merriam-Webster's dictionary, a narcissist is extremely self-centered with an exaggerated sense of self-importance marked by or characteristic of excessive admiration of oneself. This seems to fit Madoff perfectly and is indicative of self-serving behavior with total disregard for the interests of investors.

Soltes discusses the Madoff affair and conversation with students in his MBA and executive education courses to help them realize something important about themselves: knowing the difference between right and wrong is not sufficient to avoid falling into the behavioral traps people can face when under pressure to succeed.[181] One must have the intent to act in accordance with ethical standards and the moral courage to follow through on ethical intent with ethical action.

Digging deeper, why did Madoff do what he did? It seems the trappings of personal success motivated his actions. Perhaps all the expensive shopping trips, hotel stays, and yacht club memberships created an aura of success. However, as time went by, he needed more and more money to feed his habit. One's success can be fleeting when it is achieved on the backs of others.

What about Madoff's happiness and sense of well-being? Clearly, it was fleeting and based on ethical blindness. The Ponzi scheme set up a scenario where Madoff needed to scam more and more investors to show alleged high returns and encourage additional investors to give him their money. His happiness was linked to perpetuating the scheme and illustrates how egoistic decision making can hasten the slide down the ethical slippery slope. It also shows how achieving happiness may occur in the short run, but not in the long run, which is the best standard of ethical behavior.

Jeffrey Wigand: Putting Public Trust over Self-Interest

Not everyone engages in wrongful behavior. Some people do the right thing for the right reasons. Jeffrey Wigand is one such person. Wigand is a hero who put the interests of the those who smoked cigarettes ahead of his own interests and paid the price. You may not know about him. Yet, in 1996, Wigand changed forever the way cigarettes were sold by publicly disclosing the unsafe aspects of nicotine and its addictive effects.

Wigand was a biochemist and researcher who discovered that smoking cigarettes could be hazardous to our health. He is the insider who blew the whistle on the tobacco company Brown & Williamson that had added ingredients to nicotine for years to make it more addictive.

Being an ethical person can come at a cost. Wigand faced an ethical dilemma: Should he go public and tell what he knew about the dangers of cigarette smoking, or should he remain silent, as his employer wanted, and honor the confidentiality agreement he had signed that entitled him to a lucrative severance package? He agonized over what was the right thing to do. Ultimately, his conscience got the better of him and he went public. As the dangers of smoking became more apparent, Wigand contacted the television show *60 Minutes* and told his story to the world.

Just imagine how many people's lives were better off because of what Wigand did. How the warnings about smoking changed their behavior and strengthened their ability to meet physiological and safety needs. Wigand's story is one in which a person of good will acted in a way that improved the lives of others and whose actions were motivated by ethical reasons. He saw a moral duty to inform the public and acted to do so even at great cost to himself.

What were the effects on Wigand? Sure, he was thought of as a hero of sorts, but he had to endure vicious attacks by Brown & Williamson to discredit him. The company had gotten private records from the Louisville courtroom where one of many lawsuits brought by states against Brown & Williamson would be heard. Once it became clear Wigand was going public, he and his family received death threats and his character was attacked. Yet, he persisted in getting the story out there. Amid lawsuits, countersuits, and an extensive smear campaign orchestrated by the company, he lost his job, his family, his privacy, and his reputation. He was divorced and his daughters went to live with his ex-wife.

After leaving the company, Wigand couldn't find a job in the industry and wound up teaching at a high school. His $300,000 a year salary at Brown & Williamson became $30,000 a year teaching chemistry and Japanese. He became a key witness in a singular legal attempt by seven states to seek reimbursement of Medicaid expenses resulting from smoking-related illnesses.[182]

According to an exposé in 2002 by Chuck Salter for *Fast Company*, Wigand said he doesn't like to be called a whistle-blower because it suggests that you're a tattletale or that you're somehow disloyal. Wigand claims he wasn't disloyal but was loyal to a higher order of ethical responsibility. He simply told the truth about how Brown & Williamson misled consumers about the highly addictive nature of nicotine, how it ignored research indicating that some of its additives used to improve flavor caused cancer, how the company encoded and hid documents that could be used against it.[183]

Wigand is an example of someone who did what was ethically honorable but then suffered greatly for it. Still, we believe his life is better for it despite the suffering he incurred. Feeling good about one's actions builds self-esteem, enhances meaningfulness, and can become a transcendent experience because society is better off for one's moral courage. Wigand certainly was all that, and even though his actions caused him great personal heartache, this is how he responded to a question from Mike Wallace on *60 Minutes* about whether he wished he hadn't told the truth: "There are times I wish I hadn't done it. But there are times that I feel compelled to do it. If you asked me if I would do it again or if I think it's worth it, yeah, I think it's worth it. I think in the end people will see the truth."[184]

Edward Snowden: Does the End Justify the Means?

The Edward Snowden affair is a classic example of whether the end justifies the means. The main ethical issue in the Snowden case can be expressed as follows: When is it ethically appropriate to violate the law to act for a greater purpose?

Exhibit 4.1

Edward Snowden

In June 2013, computer expert, former CIA systems administrator, and government contractor Edward Snowden released confidential government documents about massive electronic surveillance by the National Security Agency to collect vast amounts of information about the telephone calls made by millions of Americans, as well as emails and social media posts.

In an interview with Glenn Greenwald of *The Guardian*, a British newspaper, Snowden explained why he became a whistleblower: "The NSA has built an infrastructure that allows it to intercept almost everything. . . . If I wanted to see your emails or your wife's phone, all I have to do is use intercepts. I can get your emails, passwords, phone records, credit cards. I don't want to live in a society that does these sort of things. . . . I do not want to live in a world where everything I do and say is recorded. That is not something I am willing to support or live under."

Snowden believed the public had a right to know about the secretive program. Others, including Eric Holder, attorney general at the time, called him a criminal. A federal criminal complaint was filed charging Snowden with violating the Espionage Act of 1917, for theft of government property.

Snowden had fled the country before disclosing the information, ostensibly to avoid prosecution. He wound up in Russia, where he stated in an online chat that although he desired to return to the United States, he wouldn't do so for fear that he would not get a fair trial.

Over time, some in the public softened their views about Snowden as it became increasingly clear that the massive amounts of data collected by the government interfered with privacy rights of Americans.

In a phone interview with *The Guardian* on June 4, 2018, five years after leaking NSA data, Snowden said he has no regrets. He is satisfied with the way his revelations of mass surveillance has rocked governments, intelligence agencies, and major internet companies. Although some privacy campaigners have expressed disappointment with how things have developed, Snowden believes the most important change is public awareness.[185]

Put another way: Did Snowden's goal of informing the public about threats to their privacy justify the way he leaked information about the National Security Agency's surveillance program? The key ethical questions are: What was Snowden's moral obligation? Did he violate that obligation by leaking confidential NSA information to the public? Did more good consequences than bad ones come to the public because of his actions? These are not easy questions to answer because it depends on what you believe to be Snowden's moral obligation.

Exhibit 4.1 summarizes the facts of the case to refresh your memory.

What Did Snowden Hope to Accomplish?

Snowden explained what he had hoped to accomplish on May 19, 2015, during an interview for a nationally syndicated radio program, "Philosophy Talk." One question was whether he was reluctant to "break the law." Discussing his personal motivations for leaking the NSA documents, Snowden said he was motivated more by "self-interest" than altruism because he felt that his actions would improve societal well-being by revealing and ultimately dismantling the NSA's metadata collection programs. He stated there are moral obligations to act when the law no longer reflects the morality of the society it governs, which is another way of saying sometimes it's necessary to violate the law for the greater good.[186]

Did Snowden Have a Choice in How to Act?

Did the end goal of disclosing confidential NSA surveillance practices justify the way in which Snowden made that disclosure? One way to evaluate the means used to stop the NSA program is whether Snowden had a choice. Was there another way to get the information out there? Snowden insisted that he had tried to use internal channels to make complaints before taking the documents to the press but that he was not successful, thanks to a broken system. However, it does not appear that he exhausted all alternatives before going public. He could have informed the Inspector General of the NSA, the U.S. Office of Government Ethics, or a congressional oversight committee.

Snowden assumed blowing the whistle wouldn't do any good because others before him tried it and suffered the consequences. He believed the culture at NSA was very insular. It did not promote transparency. Still, did that relieve him of his obligation to make every effort possible to resolve the matter internally before going public? Whistleblowers have a moral obligation to do what they can by reporting wrongdoing internally, as did Jeffrey Wigand, and using the established systems before going external and reporting the matter to an outside source. However, when those systems are broken, it's up to each whistle-blower to decide what their moral obligation is.

Snowden had a professional obligation to the NSA to protect its data-gathering system, which was confidential. Would it have done any good to honor that commitment or was it more important to get the word out and protect the public interest? For that let's examine the ethical issues using the decision-making process described in Figure 1.1 in Chapter 1.

Ethical Awareness

Recognize the ethical issues

Did the public have a right to know about the NSA's collection of personal, private information? How should his obligation to the NSA have factored into the decision? What were his ethical obligations? Did Snowden violate his ethical obligation by leaking confidential NSA surveillance data to the public?

Identify the ethical values

Confidentiality. Sensitive NSA data should not be publicly disclosed without the permission of the agency.

Privacy. The NSA accessed personal information about citizens without their knowledge.

Honesty. Snowden disclosed practices that actually existed. He didn't lie about them or deceive others about it.

Loyalty. Snowden had a loyalty obligation to the NSA to live by its rules, to protect sensitive information. However, the loyalty obligation is not absolute when staying silent harms the public good.

Integrity. It took moral courage for Snowden to put himself at risk to protect the public. His intentions were good, but the way he went about it could be questioned.

Law abiding. Some have argued that even if Snowden was legally culpable, he was not ethically responsible because the law allowing personal data collection itself was unjust and unconstitutional. Ethical people often go beyond the law when they believe a law is unjust. Snowden felt this way, but the ethical question is, What if everyone in a similar position went public? This might cause major disruptions to government programs and raises the question of whether there is a better way to handle it.

Ethical Judgment

Identify and analyze the alternatives

Virtue

Virtue theory examines whether a person did the right thing, in the right way, for the right reason. It all depends on whether we believe disclosing the confidential information was the right thing to do. What was Snowden's intent? It was to protect the public. He wasn't looking to sell the secrets for financial gain. It does seem, however, that his intentions may have been, at least in part, to embarrass the NSA because he collected confidential information over a relatively long period of time; it wasn't a spur-of-the-moment decision. The question from a virtue perspective is, Did Snowden act rashly by disclosing the data, an extreme of acting with courage? Perhaps a more measured, balanced response was warranted.

Consequentialism

Weighing the costs and benefits of Snowden's actions is difficult because much is unknown about the harms and little can be done to weigh the benefits. Still, we can look at the consequences of his actions in a general way.

Benefits:

- Public awareness of NSA's data collection program.

- Encryption of sensitive data followed the disclosure, making sensitive information more secure.

- A more effective whistleblowing process followed the disclosure, making it easier for insiders to bring matters of concern to higher levels of NSA.

- Public debate about where the line should be drawn between privacy and surveillance is ongoing.
- U.S. Congress passed the Freedom Act in 2015, curbing the mass collection of phone data.

Costs:

- The Pentagon estimated the costs to revamp systems, improve data collection controls, and so forth will be in the billions.
- Ongoing damage assessment by intelligence agencies.
- Embarrassing disclosures that the NSA system hacked foreign governments and some foreign leaders.
- Personal costs to Snowden, who left the United States to avoid prosecution and has been in Russia since 2013. He gave up a comfortable life for an uncertain future.

A rule utilitarian perspective is interesting in this case. It would hold that an act is correct when it corresponds to rules whose preservation increases the mass of happiness in the world. Did Snowden's actions maximize happiness or pleasure while minimizing unhappiness or pain? Of course, we would have to know more over a longer period of time to answer this question. We may never know how many people were affected or how the data breach harmed them. It does seem, in a general sense, that we are better off knowing than not knowing about the data collection program. Transparency can be a great disinfectant when corruption is involved, and we could conclude the NSA's program was corrupt. Freedom of information access is a democratic value.

Kantian Rights

Did the NSA have a right to expect Snowden to maintain the confidentiality of the data collection program no matter what? On the one hand, Snowden had a moral duty to protect sensitive NSA data. On the other hand, we could say that he had a moral duty to do something about the illegal collection of the data that was hidden from the public. One duty is absolute; the other is implied. A universality perspective might have led Snowden to reason that he should take that action which should be universalized: anyone in his situation should put the public good over a professional obligation even if it means violating the law. We could turn this around and say anyone in his situation should maintain the confidentiality of the sensitive information else top-level security data could be disclosed without limitation and compromise government actions to keep such data out of the hands of bad actors.

Ethical Intent

Decide on a course of action

As previously mentioned, Snowden intended to put a stop to the illegal NSA data collection program that was harmful to the public and violated people's privacy rights. His motives seemed good, but the way he went about it seemed designed to cause maximum harm to the NSA and U.S. government.

Why didn't he use the internal reporting process or go to oversight groups? Snowden was greatly influenced by what happened to Thomas Drake, a major surveillance whistle-blower who preceded Snowden. Drake had been indicted under the Espionage Act for disclosing illegal activities, waste, and mismanagement at the NSA. All charges were dropped except that Drake pled to one misdemeanor count for exceeding authorized use of a computer in gathering incriminating evidence to support his case. Snowden may have seen what happened to Drake, realized he was doing the same thing, and then decided that blowing the whistle to the NSA Inspector General or other bodies would be a waste of time.

Ethical Action

Check yourself and behave ethically

We know what Snowden did and why, and we can assume that he first "checked" his behavior before acting. He must have considered how he would feel if his disclosures made the front page of the newspaper because that was his intent: to seek out reporters from *The Guardian* to get his story out there and get broad exposure.

We really can't measure the damage done by Snowden's disclosures nor can we determine the benefits to society. My feeling is Snowden dismissed the means of alerting the public to the privacy concerns as a "casualty of war," so to speak, rather than as an element of ethical behavior directed toward the end goal—to make the public aware of NSA's surveillance program. In his own words, his intentions were self-serving yet to protect society. He invoked the *kill the messenger* defense: Don't blame me for the government's wrongdoing. I'm just the bearer of the bad news.

All things considered, it could be concluded that Snowden did the right thing in the wrong way but for the right reasons. However, if he did it the wrong way, then it brings into question whether it was the right thing to do. I'll leave it to you to make the final determination.

One final thought. It's interesting to consider whether Snowden's actions added meaning to his life, helped him to self-actualize, and provided a transcendent experience in that they were motivated (according to Snowden) by an intention to protect the public interest.

Interestingly, about half of Americans (49%) said the release of classified information served the public interest, whereas 44 percent said it harmed the public interest, according to a Pew Research Center survey taken shortly after the disclosure. At the same time, 54 percent of the public said the government should pursue a criminal case against the person responsible for the leaks. Clearly, the American public was divided. It's possible that a survey taken today might show different results with the passage of time and a renewed perspective.

Conclusion

The purpose of this chapter is to show how the decisions of businesses and individual decision makers can affect the public welfare. In many cases, our well-being is inextricably linked to those decisions and our happiness hangs in the balance. One thing for sure is businesses and individual decision makers should take a broader, societal perspective in making decisions and not decide based solely, or even largely, on self-interest. These are not easy issues because, as we learned in the Snowden case, societal interest can cut both ways.

We could say that both Jeffrey Wigand and Edward Snowden sought greater meaning in life by blowing the whistle on wrongdoing in the interests of serving the public good. We could add that in each case a feeling of self-worth resulted from their actions. Whereas the public held Wigand in high esteem for his actions, the jury is still out on the Snowden affair.

In the next chapter, we'll look at a variety of decisions you might face in everyday life and how they might directly affect your happiness, meaning in life, and pursuit of self-actualization.

CHAPTER 5

Everyday Ethics

Ethics is knowing the difference between what you have a right to do and what is right to do.

—Potter Stewart

Potter Stewart (1915–1985) was an associate justice of the U.S. Supreme Court and known for his contributions to criminal justice reform and civil rights. His quote reflects the simple truth that although you may have a right to do something— it breaks no law—that doesn't mean it's right to do. Circumstances differ, claims on ethical behavior change, and the reasons for acting are unique to each situation. Whether you have a right to do something depends on your moral duties to others.

What ethical dilemmas did you encounter today? Yesterday? A week ago? Last month? Think about it. How did you handle each matter? In retrospect, did you handle it the way you expected to handle it, or did something get in the way? Do you think reading this book would have made a difference? I hope so, even if for no other reason than you are now better able to spot ethical issues when they arise. My philosophy is to make every day an ethical day. Let's briefly review where we are at this stage of the book. We are aware that our actions affect others. We know that the Golden Rule provides a generalized moral principle that tells us how to treat others. We may not be able to resolve all ethical conflicts using the Golden Rule because ethical values can conflict, such as being faithful to our employment obligations versus being honest with the public, situations faced by Jeffrey Wigand and Edward Snowden. We follow a prescribed decision-making process to be sure we have addressed the important points. We use ethical reasoning to think through the best way to deal with such matters. We check ourselves before acting to be certain we feel comfortable with our decision. We act!

Following these steps provides a pathway to happiness and greater meaning in life, which are the end goals of a life well lived. The process ensures that we have given due consideration to the ethics of alternative courses of action in seeking to enhance our well-being.

Applying Maslow's hierarchy of needs to our end goals of happiness and meaning, the means to achieve them, and the needs that are satisfied by our behavior leads to the relationships shown in Table 5.1.

Table 5.1

Relationship between End Goals in Life and Means to Achieve Them

Means to Achieve End Goals	Need Satisfied	End Goal
Care for one's own interests	Physiological and safety needs	Happiness
Developing meaningful relationships	Belongingness and love needs	
Emphasizing good outcomes over bad ones	Esteem needs	
Peak experiences	Aesthetic needs	Meaning
Finding meaning in life	Self-actualization	
Look beyond ourselves and act in ways that benefit others	Transcendence	

As you read this chapter, you can evaluate your thought process from an ethical perspective in the context of a variety of everyday occurrences. By working through a series of hypothetical situations, you will learn to apply your knowledge, build moral muscle memory, and gain confidence in dealing with these and other matters where right and wrong, good and bad are at stake.

Short Exercises

The following short exercises describe everyday occurrences that raise ethical issues that can be resolved without the benefit of a formal decision-making process.

The ATM Machine

You are inside a vestibule waiting for the customer in front of you to complete her transaction at an ATM machine. She takes her money and leaves. No one is behind you in line. You quickly notice she left a $20 bill. You decide to keep the $20. Was that wrong of you?

Keeping the money is like stealing. You took something that wasn't yours. You should have attempted to catch her before she got too far away and give her the $20. Doing so illustrates the Golden Rule in action and its shows you have ethical intent. How would you feel if you were the one who left the $20 behind?

Missing Work

You manage a group of six employees. One day one of those employees calls in sick. Later that day you notice the employee posted photos on Instagram that were taken at a restaurant. What would you do?

It's possible the pictures were taken on another day but posted the sick day, so it's best to speak to the employee about the incident. Firing the employee seems hasty and unjust and it might lead to legal action for wrongful termination. The virtue of self-control is instructive here. Avoid the extremes of behavior. Don't overreact and fire her on the spot; don't shy away from discussing the matter. Find a way to moderate your behavior and deal with the matter fairly. Other employees will take their cue from what you decide to do and why.

Workplace Harassment

Your boss comes on to you at work. He constantly asks about your dating life and if you're seeing anyone. He regularly stares at you. His behavior makes you feel uncomfortable. But you are up for a promotion and he has the final say. What would you do?

Sexual harassment exists when the unwanted behavior is severe enough to affect your work or create a hostile work environment. Given that the behavior is constant and regular, it's probably safe to say it is sexual harassment. You should always first discuss the matter with your boss and inform him that you are uncomfortable. It's possible your boss has an ethical blind spot and is unaware his behavior is offensive. Ignoring it until you get the promotion doesn't make the problem go away, and your boss may even exhibit more aggressive behavior toward you now that he's done something nice for you.

Posting Critical Comments About an Employer

You work for a demanding boss who just scolded you for taking ten extra minutes for lunch. You feel embarrassed, especially because the scolding was in front of other employees. You explained that your child is sick and the nanny called to let you know. Your boss doesn't seem to care. You posted critical comments about your boss on Facebook during your next break. Now, you're wondering whether it was the right thing to do.

Do you have a right to do it? The National Labor Relations Board has ruled that critical comments about an employer are protected conduct when it involves concerted activity. If the comment was an isolated statement made by one employee, then it would qualify as a "personal gripe," which is not protected. If other employees comment on your post agreeing and disagreeing with you, this constitutes concerted action.

Was it right to do? Assuming other employees commented, what you did is legal. However, this is a situation where what you have a right to do and what is right to do differ. Why antagonize the boss? If you have a gripe, talk to him or her in private. It might be helpful here to ask yourself how you would feel if your boss posted critical comments about your work habits online.

Sexting

Sexting is the act of sending sexually explicit material or explicit photographs or videos through text messages.

Consider the following. Karen just turned twenty-one and found her true love. She's never felt this way before. One day her boyfriend, Alan, takes a sexually explicit photograph of her with her permission. They shared it between themselves until Karen ended the relationship. Alan was hurt by the breakup, so he posted the picture on Instagram. Did Alan have a right to do so? Was it ethical?

Alan may have had a right to post it unless the social media site prohibits such photos. However, it wasn't an ethical act because it was motivated by revenge. Most states have laws against nonconsensual disclosure of sexually explicit images and videos, or revenge porn. Karen would have to give consent for it to be legally shared. She can contact Instagram and it may take the photo down, but it may be too late—the pictures may have been seen or downloaded by others.

Using the decision-making concept of "checking yourself," a good rule to follow is: Don't put anything on the internet that you don't want to appear forever. Alan should use this perspective in deciding what to do by looking at the situation from Karen's point of view. This means following the Golden Rule, which would lead Alan not to post the photo. Empathy and compassion for another are good ethical values to adhere to in this kind of situation.

Spending Time with Family and Friends

Joyce is an associate attorney who has worked for five years at the same firm. She hopes to become a junior partner this year. Her mentor has urged her to increase her billable hours. Joyce is considering working beyond the current forty-eight-hour level (8 hours per day for 6 days a week) but is being pressured by her husband to spend more time with him and the kids. Should Joyce increase her work hours?

The issue here is what makes Joyce happy. She may derive meaning from work but at the expense of happiness at home. Spending more time with her husband and the kids satisfies her need for love and belongingness. It can stimulate greater growth and development as a parent. Joyce's decision is unique to her situation, so the response is personal. An interesting approach is to ask: What would she want etched in stone at her gravesite: *Here lies Joyce, who wished she spent more time at work* or *Here lies Joyce, loving wife and mother?*

Staging an Intervention

Billy has been addicted to alcohol for many years. He can barely hold down a job before the alcoholism causes him to be fired. His behavior has become more erratic and sometimes hostile to his wife. It's gotten so bad that his wife and children dread it when he comes home. They are considering staging an intervention with other family members to describe to Billy how his behavior is affecting their lives. Is the intervention a good idea?

Staging an intervention when someone is addicted to drugs or alcohol shows you care about that person, can empathize with what they are going through, and want to help them to help themselves. Billy's actions have caused unhappiness for his wife and children. The intervention is a good idea but should be planned in advance and only after Billy has been informed. Otherwise, he may react defensively and the message won't get through. The benefits of an intervention—becoming sober, being a loving husband and father, gaining self-esteem, and achieving greater happiness and meaning in life—outweigh the potential cost that Billy may resist or that it may not work. Even if the intervention doesn't work, the family is no worse off for trying. Finally, they could ask: How would they feel if they didn't stage the intervention and Billy went further downhill?

Lying on a Résumé

Cheryl has been unemployed for six months. She's having difficulty providing for her family with just unemployment money. It's created a strain in the family dynamic. Cheryl decides to look for a full-time job that will double the amount she receives from unemployment. She shows her résumé to a friend, who suggests stretching the dates she worked for a prior employer by one year to cover up a one-year gap in the dates of employment. She doesn't think an employer would realize what she's done because no one at the prior employer is listed as a reference. Is this a good idea?

Cheryl may think distorting the dates of employment is justifiable and, if she gets the job, it would bring happiness to herself and the family by alleviating financial pressures. Perhaps it would, but Cheryl needs to take a broader perspective and ask: What if the prospective employer questions her on the dates of employment or contacts the prior employer? She's already been dishonest by adding in the extra year and now has to cover up her mistake or admit to lying. Lying on her résumé puts her in the position of sliding down the ethical slippery slope if questioned about it.

Adding an extra year to her employment record and deciding it's justifiable is rationalizing an unethical act. It reflects an end justifies the means approach to ethical decision making because Cheryl is willing to do whatever is necessary to get the high-paying job. However, she has a moral duty to be honest with the prospective employer and should not want to start an employment relationship with a lie. Imagine if everyone lied on their résumé about dates of employment, adding a job they didn't have, or embellishing their experience. This would put Cheryl in a weaker position in getting the job. The universality perspective provides good guidance here.

Covering Up for a Boss

Your boss asks you to cover for him on an expense report by saying you were at a business dinner when you weren't so that he can get reimbursed for his wife's meal. The company reimbursement policy only allows for your boss's meal and the business guest's. Should you sign the report?

Signing the report is wrong. It violates company policy and, if you sign it, you become part of a fraud and the cover-up.

Why would anyone compromise their integrity by signing the report? It could be to keep your boss happy; get on his good side; or because you feel intimidated by the boss, much like Betty Vinson did in the WorldCom fraud.

Often, when a boss asks an employee to cover up their misdeed, it's explained as being standard practice at the company and the employee needs to be a team player. Maybe this is true. If so, the employee should ask whether this is the kind of company they want to work for—one that asks them to cover up a lie or fraudulent act.

Putting aside the issue of whether you get caught, if you sign off, then it's more likely your boss will ask you to do it again in the future or to cover up another misdeed. It's an "I gotcha" moment where you have begun the slide down the ethical slippery slope and it won't be easy to reverse course and reclaim the moral high road.

Reporting Crime

Some in the community are up in arms after a police officer is found not guilty in the shooting of an unarmed civilian. The video of the incident clearly shows the civilian was trying to give up. Following the verdict, irate citizens looted a local electronics store, taking laptops, tablets, and smartphones and destroying property. You know this because you were one in a crowd of people outside the store witnessing the crime. You also know two of the looters. You want to come forward but fear the reprisals. You remain silent, hoping that others will come forward instead. Was this the proper decision?

No. This is an example of the bystander effect, where you remained silent by rationalizing that someone else would come forward. A responsible citizen sees it as a civic duty to come forward. If you had owned the store, the likelihood is you would want the witness to come forward, bring the guilty parties to justice, and recover the stolen property.

Dumping Toxic Waste

Late one night you were walking by a local stream when you noticed a person dump something into the water outside a manufacturing plant. You couldn't see what it was, but at a later date the residents around the stream started to get sick from the contaminated water. The authorities were investigating whether the dumping was done by the local manufacturing plant. Should you report what you observed?

Yes. Reporting the matter is a responsible act, done out of civic duty, and contributes to the well-being of the community. Reporting it would likely be hailed as a meaningful act and you would be held in high esteem. By reporting it, you will likely feel good about yourself, feel pride in your actions, feel self-fulfilled, and save others from getting ill. On the other hand, ignoring it means you lost the opportunity to improve health conditions in the community and hold the guilty accountable for their actions. Reporting the dumping can be a transcendent act because you are motivated by the betterment of society.

The Lost Briefcase

A customer paid for his fare and got out of your taxi. You went to lunch. Later, you noticed that the customer left his briefcase in the taxi. You opened the briefcase to see if you could find the name and address of the owner. You did. Much to your surprise, there were valuable documents and thousands of dollars in cash in the case, too. What would you do: (1) return the briefcase; or (2) discard the briefcase and documents but keep the cash?

Returning the briefcase is the right thing to do and it should be done for the right reason—as a virtuous act, not for a reward. Can we feel happy about returning the case? Yes, because it shows we care about others, and that's the essence of ethical behavior. Can it add meaning to our life? Yes, because we would experience feelings of self-worth and be held in high esteem. The Golden Rule applies here. You would want the briefcase returned to you if you had left it in a taxi. So, you should reciprocate.

This exact situation occurred on December 4, 2018, when a taxi driver in Thailand returned more than 300,000 baht (Thai currency), which equaled $9,800 in cash, to an American tourist who had left it in the cab. The cabbie found the tourist at the airport and gave him the money. The tourist thanked the driver for returning his lost bag and praised him for his honesty.[187]

A different cabbie might have thought it was unlikely the passenger would have been able to track him down, so it would be worth the risk of keeping the cash. However, as discussed in Chapter 4, a risk analysis is often not the most ethical way to decide what to do. Remember, ethics is about what we do when no one is looking.

Ethical Dilemmas

We analyze the following cases using the ethical decision-making process depicted in Figure 1.1 in Chapter 1. Recall the components of the process: recognize the ethical issues and identify the ethical values (ethical awareness); identify and analyze the ethics of the alternatives (ethical judgment); decide on a course of action (ethical intent); and check yourself and behave ethically (ethical action). In the interests of brevity, not all of the steps and not all the ethical reasoning methods are covered in each case.

Ghosting in the Workplace

In Chapter 1, we looked at ghosting in dating relationships and analyzed what Sally should do after ghosting Bill after two dates. Here, we examine the ethical issue of ghosting in the context of interviewing for a job. First, let's look at some of the issues surrounding the acceptability of ghosting in the interview process.

Ghosting in the workplace is when a candidate abruptly disengages from the interview process without explanation. Ghosting occurs in different ways, including not keeping employers informed of a decision, not showing up for the first day of work, and disappearing after accepting a job. Employers also engage in ghosting when they cease to follow up with candidates or to schedule the next steps.

A survey of job seekers by *Clutch* indicates that 41 percent believe it's reasonable to ghost a company and 32 percent believe it's reasonable for companies to ghost prospective employees.

Here are the reasons why respondents said they ghosted:

- Accepted another offer (30%)
- Never heard back from the company (23%)
- Decided the position was not a match (19%)

Of those rejected by employers in their last job search, only 21 percent were rejected over the phone, 13 percent received an email, and 36 percent were not contacted at all. *Clutch* states that employers that don't communicate with job seekers send a message that they approve of ghosting.[188]

Case

Megan is a graduating senior and is interviewing for her first job. She's gone through interviews at five companies and is anxiously awaiting the responses. She gets her first offer and verbally commits to taking the job. No other offers or rejections come for two weeks, after which she gets an offer that is too good to refuse. It's the better of the two offers and from her preferred employer. Megan has decided to accept that offer. She asks for your advice in deciding what to do next: (1) inform the first employer of her decision and inform the others; (2) inform the first employer of her decision but don't inform the others; (3) do not inform any of the employers of her decision.

Ethical Awareness

Recognize the ethical issues

Does Megan have an ethical obligation to inform the other employers of her decision?

Identify the ethical values

> *Honesty.* Not informing the employers is dishonest. It's a lie by omission.

> *Caring and concern.* While Megan has no legal obligation to inform the employers, informing them shows concern for the fact they may be interviewing other candidates and knowing about Megan's decision helps them along.

> *Responsibility.* Although Megan has no legal obligation to inform the employers, doing so is a responsible act. It shows she is aware that her actions affect the employers in their search for candidates. She has a special responsibility to inform the first employer because it made an offer, held a position open for her, and will need to fill it once informed of Megan's decision. Failing to inform this

employer means a position that would otherwise be closed is really open because Megan plans to renege on the offer. The other employers rely on Megan's honesty to facilitate their recruitment process.

Legal versus ethical. Just because there is no legal obligation to inform the first employer (unless Megan signed an employment contract), it's the right thing to do as explained below.

Ethical Judgment

Identify and analyze the alternatives

1. Inform all employers.

   Informing the first employer shows respect for the fact it offered Megan a job. Using utilitarianism, Megan's thought process might proceed as follows:

   Benefits: Even though it may be blindsided by her decision, the first employer will respect Megan's actions, especially if that employer has been ghosted by other candidates. It's better to know than not to know. It also helps the other employers in their decision-making process because they know not to count on Megan to fill the position.

   Harms: There may be some harm to Megan's reputation for trustworthiness in reneging on an offer, but not informing the first employer makes matters worse.

2. Inform the first employer, but not the others.

   The benefits and harms of informing the first employer are the same as discussed above. The consequences of not informing the other employers is discussed next.

Benefits: There aren't any benefits of not informing the other employers except that it may be easier for Megan to avoid such conversations. If so, she can simply send an email saying: "Thanks for the opportunity to interview with your firm. I want to let you know that I've accepted another position."

Harms: The other employers may be in the midst of making offers, and not knowing about Megan's decision adds a level of uncertainty in deciding who should receive the offer. Other candidates may lose the opportunity to compete for that position if these employers assume Megan is still interested in the position.

3. Do not inform any of the employers.

There are no tangible benefits to this decision.

Harms: It's wrong not to inform the first employer. It went to the trouble of making an offer and is counting on Megan showing up the first day. If she doesn't, the employer needs to reopen the search to fill that position, so the sooner it knows, the better. It will be in a significantly weaker position if Megan doesn't inform them because the interviewing process has been ongoing and it may lose the opportunity to sign up other employees. Other graduating seniors may be in a weakened position if employers have kept a position open for Megan.

Megan might ask: How would she feel if an employer made her an offer, she accepted it, and then the employer pulled the offer without telling her?

Megan may rationalize that she's been ghosted before, so there's nothing wrong in turning the table on the employers. There is an old expression that says two wrongs don't make a right, which applies in this situation.

Kantian ethics emphasizes the good will or moral reasons for acting. What is Megan's motivation if she doesn't inform any of the employers? It seems to be a selfish act without concern for the well-being of the employers in the interview process or students waiting to see whether they get a job offer. On the other hand, informing all the employers shows good faith and is an act she would want the employers to take if Megan was waiting for offers. Megan should ask whether she would want employers and other students to engage in ghosting (universality perspective). If that occurs, then the recruitment process would be confusing, to say the least, and counterproductive.

Ethical Intent

Decide on a course of action

Megan should think carefully about her intention in deciding what to do. How does she want to be known by the employers? Does she want to be respected for her decision? If so, she should inform all the employers. Failing to inform the employers won't make her happy, although it might make things more comfortable. However, it's not worth putting her reputation in jeopardy for expediency. If she values honesty, Megan would inform the first and other employers because to do otherwise is to lie by omission.

Ethical Action

Check yourself

Megan might ask the following questions:

> How would she feel if her decision to renege and not to inform the first employer was made public and everyone knew about it? Would she feel proud to defend it?

> How would she feel if she ghosted the first employer, which motivated that company to contact the university and lodge a complaint about her behavior? Would she be able to defend it to a recruiting counselor or adviser?

> How would she feel if she failed to inform the first employer, other students at her university lost out in the position, and those students took to social media to criticize her? Would she feel embarrassed? How would she respond to the negative comments?

Behave ethically

Megan should treat the other employers the same way she would wish to be treated in a reverse ghosting situation.

The first employer is not likely to be happy about her decision to renege on the offer and not to inform it. Megan would not be held in high esteem. A meaningful act is one that creates pride and feelings of self-worth. It's hard to imagine Megan feeling this way while not informing the first employer of her decision.

Is a selfish act ever an ethical act? An egoist might say so, but Megan's failure to inform employers misses the mark on basic ethical standards, which is to consider how one's actions affect others. Perhaps her motivation to not inform is driven by making her life less complicated, in which case she lacks moral courage. The bottom line is the employers have a right to know of her decision. No one ever said being ethical is easy. In fact, Michael Josephson has written about "Ethics—Easier Said Than Done."[189]

Catfishing on the Internet

A catfish, the Urban Dictionary says, is someone who pretends to be someone they're not by using social media sites to create false identities, particularly to pursue deceptive online romances. Catfishing has become easier and more pervasive with the increasing popularity of online dating apps like Tinder and Bumble. It's been speculated that 20 percent of Tinder profiles are fake.[190]

Case

Barry routinely works ten hours a day, six days a week. He doesn't have time to go to the bars or other places to find a date, so he uses an online dating app to connect. Barry knows a lot of people create false personas online, including a fake photo, and provide inaccurate or incomplete information about themselves. He's considering doing the same to attract more favorable dating partners.

What would you do if you were in Barry's place?

Ethical Awareness

Recognize the ethical issues

Does Barry have an ethical obligation to be completely honest in posting personal information on the dating site?

Identify the ethical values

Honesty. Barry would be lying if he posts a false profile online. Creating a false profile online is a lie by commission because Barry knowingly posts false information. He might dismiss it by rationalizing that he isn't harming anyone and could become truthful if the communications lead to an actual date. Moreover, he may reason "everyone does it." Indeed, surveys have shown a high percentage of users do lie.[191] However, being honest does not depend on others' actions. It depends on our good will and intention not to deceive another for our self-serving interests.

Trustworthiness. It's difficult to develop a trusting relationship once the other party learns of the falsehood. The other party might ask: If he lied about this, what else might he have lied about? Can I rely on his word? The lying party's credibility would be harmed once the truth is known.

Integrity. A person of integrity tells the truth regardless of the personal costs. Exaggerating important information to increase the likelihood of making a match is unprincipled behavior. If a connection is made, an inauthentic relationship begins. Claiming that everyone does it reflects an end justifies the means approach to decision making. Lying on a dating profile to make a more favorable match illustrates a rationalization for an unethical act. We should not base our actions on the lowest ethical common denominator. A principled person does what is right precisely because it is the right thing to do.

Ethical Judgment

Identify and analyze the alternatives

The main issue is whether Barry should knowingly post false and/or misleading personal information on the dating app. The alternatives are simple: do it or don't do it. The Golden Rule is instructive here. Barry should consider how he would feel if the roles were reversed. The truth is, Barry might not care; he may assume everyone lies and he'll discover the truth once they meet in person. Maybe so, but what if the other party lied about more than their physical appearance? What if they claimed to be a millionaire but were homeless? Where do we draw the line between a "harmless" lie and one that is a game-changer?

Barry should consider that he would be misleading the dating partner by posting false information and that it may backfire on him. The other party may feel deceived once the truth is known, and it may have consequences even after the relationship begins if, for example, he lied about his financial resources. Hypothetically, if it becomes known that he isn't a millionaire but is just making ends meet, an otherwise successful relationship may fall apart. He would have become invested in the relationship, and losing someone he cares about could be devastating.

A post on the Mindless Professor titled "On the Philosophy of Catfishing" examines the practice from a Kantian perspective. Kant's ethics forbids all lying in all circumstances because our actions are morally correct only if we can universalize the act. We have a moral obligation to be honest with others.[192] If everyone lied in their online dating profiles, then there would be a lot of choices made based on falsehoods. Given that many relationships start out by chatting online, a lot of time and effort may be wasted once we find out the truth.

Ethical Intent

Decide on a course of action

What motivates Barry to seek out a relationship online? We can assume it's to engage in a happy, meaningful relationship. Let's examine whether posting a false profile might add happiness and meaning to Barry's life. We could argue that he'll be happy if he makes a good connection; it could lead to a meaningful relationship regardless of the deception. On the other hand, his actions may harm the other party, who may be disillusioned once they meet and get to know each other. Barry's happiness is tied to the happiness of the other party. Lying doesn't build self-esteem, which comes from another party's response to our behaviors.

Ethical Action

Check yourself

Barry should ask how he would feel if he lied about personal information, his dating partner subsequently found out, and she took to the internet to voice her displeasure. Might this affect future dating opportunities if others see the negative post online?

Behave ethically

Barry should be honest on his profile to avoid behavior that would reflect badly on his character. This is another situation where doing what is legal doesn't make it ethical. There's no law against lying on one's dating profile, but it's wrong to do because Barry would be misleading potential dating partners. One can't build self-esteem based on lies since the other party is likely to be critical of deceitful behavior.

Barry might be sacrificing the opportunity to build a meaningful relationship by lying. His need for belongingness and a loving relationship may hang in the balance.

Dating in the Workplace

According to a Harris Poll conducted from November 28 to December 20, 2017, that included a representative sample of 809 full-time workers across industries and company sizes in the U.S. private sector, 36 percent of workers reported dating a coworker. Twenty-two percent of workers have dated someone who was their boss at the time, and 30 percent of those said they dated someone who was at a higher level in the organization than they were.[193]

There appears to be a generation gap on whether dating in the workplace has positive or negative effects, according to a survey of employed millennials by Workplace Options.[194]

- 84 percent of millennials (23-39 years old as of 2019) say they would engage in romance with a coworker compared to 36 percent of Generation X workers (ages 40-54 as of 2019), and only 29 percent of baby boomers (ages 55-75 as of 2019).

- 71 percent of millennials see a workplace romance as having positive effects, such as improved performance and morale.

- 40 percent of millennials report no negative effects whatsoever from an office romance; only 10 percent of older workers shared that sentiment, meaning a majority of Americans feel more harm can be done than good.

- 54 percent say that if they had a romantic relationship with a colleague, they would share information about it with others—either friends, coworkers, or via social networks.

Case

Brenda spends a lot of time in the office with Mark, her supervisor. They work closely together and have learned much about each other. Brenda has grown fond of Mark, respects his intelligence, and knows he has the kind of influence in the office that can be helpful to her career. She also feels Mark understands her, and the demands of working sixty-hour weeks. He's also familiar with office politics, which Merriam-Webster's dictionary defines as the activities, attitudes, or behaviors that are used to get or keep power or an advantage within a business or company. Given the long hours, Brenda has been unable to develop a romantic relationship outside work.

One day Mark asks Brenda to dinner. Thinking it's work related, Brenda agrees. Mark confides that he has feelings for her that go beyond employer–employee. He asks Brenda to go to the opera on Saturday and says he has center orchestra seats for *La Bohème*, by Puccini. It's her favorite opera, and the opportunity to see it for the first time is an offer too good to refuse.

After the opera and another dinner, Mark asks Brenda to date more frequently. Brenda likes Mark a lot on a personal level and is tempted to say yes. However, she is concerned about becoming involved with someone who is her direct supervisor. The company has no policy on dating.

Should Brenda agree to the dating relationship?

Ethical Awareness

Recognize the ethical issues

Is it ethical for Brenda to date someone with authority over her in the workplace?

Identify the ethical values

Honesty. Being honest is an ethical requirement that shouldn't depend on the circumstances. Brenda should consider that she may be asked about the relationship once others discover it and fully disclosing the relationship might create problems in the office because of a perceived conflict of interest for Mark. If she fails to disclose, it is a lie by omission. If she lies when asked about it, that's a lie by commission.

Fairness. Does Brenda expect to be treated favorably by Mark because of the relationship? Others may perceive favoritism. Appearances count and it may seem to other employees that Mark treats Brenda differently because of the relationship.

Responsibility. Mark is responsible for evaluating Brenda's performance, so Brenda should ask whether she wants to put him in a position where he may have to choose between giving her a good performance evaluation because of the dating relationship or being truthful about her performance. Thinking about these issues in advance enables her to make an informed decision.

Integrity. The integrity of the performance evaluation system may be at stake if Brenda is treated more favorably than other employees. She may be given better opportunities and more room to grow in the organization.

Ethical Judgment

Identify and analyze the alternatives

Utilitarianism

Using the consequence-based approach of utilitarianism, Brenda's decision-making process might proceed as follows:

Benefits of a dating relationship: Brenda is having difficulty finding the time to date. She has feelings for Mark. A meaningful relationship may bring her happiness and has intrinsic value because we value relationships for their own sake. It's also possible she'll be given better opportunities in the workplace by dating Mark, although this should not be the motivating factor to date.

Harms of a dating relationship: Other employees may resent Brenda if it is perceived she is given favorable treatment by Mark because of the dating relationship. If she and Mark break up, can there be a "silent exit," or might Mark start treating her differently, especially if Brenda ends the relationship? Will it affect her performance evaluations? Seeing her ex and working together may be awkward, affect her performance, and lead to a hostile work environment. The possibility exists of a sexual harassment claim down the road.

Other considerations: The company has no policy on dating, so they would not be breaking any rules. However, doing what is ethical is what's most important. Ethical people do not need rules to help them distinguish right from wrong. Saying the ends of finding a good dating partner exceed the means of putting both her and Mark in a compromising position is rationalizing a questionable, if not unethical, act.

A rule utilitarian perspective is useful here: never engage in a dating relationship at work with someone who evaluates your performance.

Deontology

Does Brenda have a moral duty to avoid subordinate–superior dating relationships that may not violate company policy but that make it appear she is given favored treatment? Saying the ends of finding a good dating partner are most important violates the deontological principle that our intentions must be based on moral actions, not to satisfy some need. Playing devil's advocate, would Brenda approve of other employees getting involved with their supervisors in a dating relationship? Could she view it as a universally acceptable act? Might this unduly influence the performance evaluation system for all?

Ethical Intent

Decide on a course of action

Brenda might ask: What are her intentions in getting involved in the dating relationship with Mark? Is it to engage in a satisfying relationship? Might it bring her happiness? These are things that satisfy her needs for love and belongingness. On the other hand, Brenda must carefully consider whether her real motivation is to have Mark in her corner at work, help with office politics, and have an advantage over others in the performance evaluation system. These are not worthy motivations. They are self-serving and not in the best interests of others in the organization. Here, we could say egoistic behavior drives decision making.

To have ethical intent, Brenda must be motivated to do the right thing because it is the right thing to do. Can we say engaging in a dating relationship with your superior at work is the right thing to do? It wouldn't seem so because there are no perceptible benefits for the organization.

Ethical Action

Check yourself

This is another situation in which doing what is legal and doing what is ethical are not the same. It's legal for Mark and Brenda to date, but doing so creates an entanglement that can put one party or the other in a compromised position. Hiding the relationship would create a slippery slope condition whereby each party may have to lie about or obscure the truth to cover up their dating relationship for the sake of workplace harmony. Brenda should consider whether she would feel comfortable defending the relationship if others in the organization found out and were verbally critical of the relationship or posted critical comments online because of performance evaluation concerns.

Behave ethically

What should Brenda do? To protect her own interests, Brenda might ask Mark to discuss the matter with higher-ups in the organization to clarify they have no objection to a dating relationship. Beyond that, Mark would be wise to suggest he be removed from supervising Brenda to avoid any conflict of interest.

Fight-or-Flight Response

The *fight-or-flight response,* also known as the *acute stress response,* refers to a physiological reaction that occurs in the presence of something that causes great fear or is physically threatening, and uncertainty how best to respond.

The fight-or-flight response represents the choices that we have when faced with an emotionally or physically threatening situation. We can stand our ground and deal with it as best we can or disassociate ourselves from the situation.

Fight-or-flight situations can affect our physical and psychological well-being. We feel anxious, stressed, and maybe depressed by the circumstances. Exhibit 5.1 describes the fight-or-flight response in greater detail.

Exhibit 5.1

Fight or Flight?

The fight-or-flight response was first described in the 1920s by American physiologist Walter Cannon. Cannon realized that a chain of rapidly occurring reactions inside the body helped to mobilize the body's resources to deal with threatening circumstances. In response to acute stress, the body's sympathetic nervous system is activated with a sudden release of hormones. The sympathetic nervous system stimulates the adrenal glands, triggering the release of adrenaline, which results in an increase in heart rate, blood pressure, and breathing rate. After the threat is gone, it takes between twenty and sixty minutes for the body to return to its prearousal levels.[195]

Case

Carl and Karen have been married for several years. They have come to depend on each other for physical and emotional support. They do not have any children. Since losing his job, Carl has become more critical of Karen, who is now the sole supporter, and aggressive when differences of opinion exist. Karen is growing increasingly concerned about Carl's behavior and frequent outbursts when things don't go his way. She's spoken to Carl about her feelings, but he's been dismissive. Karen has been in therapy for the past several months considering how to handle the fight-or-flight reflex that is happening more often.

Karen is also concerned about the reactive way she is responding to Carl, making it more difficult to self-regulate her behavior. She knows something needs to be done to deal with her growing depression and questions about her self-worth. She asks: Am I good person if I choose to break away from Carl?

Ethical Awareness

Recognize the ethical issues

What is the most ethical way for Karen to deal with Carl's erratic behavior?

Identify the ethical values

Compassion and empathy. These are the most important values in this case. Karen needs to care for her own needs first and then attend to Carl's. Karen cares about Carl but is also concerned for her safety.

Responsibility. Karen needs to consider that she and Carl have been together for several years and, even though conflict exists in their relationship now, she does care about Carl. Does she have an obligation to support him through these tough times?

Ethical Judgment

Identify and analyze the alternatives

For the sake of simplicity, the two alternatives are to remain in the relationship or leave it. Of course, another and, perhaps, a better alternative is for Karen and Carl to go to couples counseling and try to resolve the issues.

Virtue

Recall that virtue is the mean between two extremes: one of excess and the other of deficiency. The virtue of self-control is important in determining how Karen reacts to Mark's behavior. Self-control requires willpower, to be in charge of our feelings and reactions to others and events, especially those outside our control. It's what we use to restrain our desires. Roy F. Baumeister likens it to self-regulation. It's the capacity to override one response and substitute another. To regulate is to change in one direction or the other based on how we deem proper behavior to be in each instance.[196]

Karen needs to regulate her response to Carl's behavior. She can react to harmful behaviors in her relationship with Carl, such as those generated by the fight-or-flight response, by overreacting and causing more stress in the relationship or by not reacting at all and ignoring her desires and impulses. Karen needs to find a balance between further antagonizing Carl and doing nothing. Remaining in the relationship and debating Carl when differences exist may provoke him to more harmful behaviors, whereas doing nothing might send the wrong signal that Karen accepts what's been going on.

Karen's feelings of self-worth are at risk. Carl has become more critical and his aggressive behavior is likely to take a toll on her self-esteem over time. This is not a good outcome for Karen because it may have long-lasting effects.

Consequentialism

1. *Remain in the relationship.* Remaining in the relation-ship takes courage because of the stressful circum-stances Karen faces. Here are the consequences of such a decision:

   Benefits: The benefits of remaining in the relationship are tied to whether she believes Carl can change. Karen might seek an intervention with friends and family to explain to Carl how his actions are affecting Karen and jeopardizing their relationship. Karen would like to be loyal to Carl, but not at the risk of her own safety.

   Harms: The costs of remaining in the relationship are that Karen will stay unhappy, lose herself in the relationship, and prevent her growth and development as a caring person. Remaining in the relationship while hoping against hope that Carl will change seems to be unrealistic. She may be jeopardizing her safety, feelings of belongingness, and need for love. She may grow to further doubt herself and her feelings of self-worth. Her ability to self-actualize may be stifled.

2. *Leave the relationship.*

  Benefits: The benefit of leaving Carl is that Karen can attend to her own physiological and safety needs while working on restoring her self-esteem. Absent any evidence to the contrary, there is no reason to believe Carl will change, and staying in the relationship may be delaying the inevitable.

  Harms: The costs of leaving Carl include the feelings of guilt for abandoning him and whether it might provoke him to more destructive behaviors.

  Other considerations: A rule utilitarian approach holds that a person should never stay in an abusive relationship when one's physical safety is at risk. Karen would have to decide whether she and Carl have reached the point of no return.

Deontology

Although the costs and benefits of alternatives for Karen are relatively clear, weighing these outcomes is not. It's hard to put a value on whether Carl can change.

  Deontology looks at whether Karen has a moral duty to remain in the relationship and work on restoring the trust between her and Carl. Karen has a moral duty to protect herself from abuse. She does not have a moral duty to put Carl's interests ahead of her own, especially when further harm may come to her.

  Under the formula of universality, Karen could ask how she would feel if other women were in the same situation? Her decision should be one that could be universalized. It would seem Karen wouldn't want others to remain in an abusive relationship unless there's ample evidence it can be turned around.

Ethical Intent

Decide on a course of action

We can assume that Karen is motivated to do the right thing; she just needs to decide what that is. We could also assume that she doesn't want to hurt Carl by her actions but must protect her own safety and well-being.

What should Karen do? Ideally, Karen should continue with the therapy, maybe even try to get Carl to go. Putting that alternative aside, she needs to get in control of her feelings and not let Carl define who she is. She should place her own happiness above all else and work on her feelings of self-worth. She doesn't want to sacrifice her well-being.

Ethical Action

Check yourself

Karen could ask how she would feel if she left Carl without trying everything to save the relationship. If the roles were reversed, wouldn't she want Carl to act that way? Alternatively, she could ask what will happen if she stays with Carl but the abuse gets worse.

Behave ethically

This is a highly personalized case and one in which the most ethical decision would be affected by other variables such as financial considerations, loyalty to another, and the commitment of Carl to change. A trial separation may be the way to go. Karen can work on her self-esteem, which seems to be affected by Carl's critical comments. She should be true to herself and clear on what she expects from Carl going forward. She needs assurances that Carl will do everything possible to change and become a more loving husband.

Ethical Debates

Ethical debates are useful because each point of view may be ethically justifiable and arguments are presented by each side to support their position. The following three cases illustrate this approach to ethical decision making. The ethical analysis is generally brief but to the point.

Should an Employee with Serious Health Problems Be Fired?

You're the manager of a nonprofit organization with ten employees. You operate in an at-will employment state where it's legal to fire anyone unless doing so violates a law, such as the Americans with Disabilities Act (ADA), under which firing someone solely because of a disability is illegal. You do not fall under the rules of the ADA, which exempts entities with fewer than fifteen employees.[197]

Ken, your supervisee, has been in charge of fund-raising for three years. One year ago, his performance started to decline from the effects of being HIV-positive. Shortly after starting treatment, Ken's work output improved, but in the past few weeks it has declined significantly—he's raised only half the money as before. He explained that he is waiting for the doctors to administer a new cocktail of drugs and expects his productivity to improve. He knows you have been considering letting him go for cause and asks not to be fired. Ken is his family's sole source of income and tells you that he has little savings because of the high cost of the treatments. You have a vested interest in the decision because your performance evaluation depends on the amount of money raised. Also, there is another employee who can step in and meet fund-raising goals. What should you as the manager do?[198]

The following analysis illustrates the use of ethical reasoning to decide on a course of action.

Consequentialism

Arguments to Retain

- You're a nonprofit and should place people over profits.

- It seems Ken's been a good employee in the past and may regain a level of proficiency after successful treatment for being HIV-positive. New treatments and a healthy lifestyle can enable individuals with HIV to live long, productive lives.

- He's the sole support of his family.

- Employee morale may suffer if he is fired.

- Even though it's legal to fire Ken, it may be the wrong thing to do from the perspective of empathy and compassion.

- If Ken is fired, it's possible he would bring a lawsuit for discrimination even though the nonprofit is not under ADA rules.

Arguments to Fire

- Less money raised means less money to provide needed services. Those receiving the services may suffer.

- Your performance is judged on the basis of the results. Retaining him may affect your position.

- There is no guarantee his performance will improve.

- You have another employee ready to step in and bring back past levels of fund-raising.

Deontology

Moral intent is most important in Kantian ethics. What would be your intent in keeping Ken? Would it be to provide every opportunity for him to recover and regain past performance? This would seem to be the humane thing to do. Alternatively, you do not have a moral duty to sacrifice fund-raising and the objectives of the nonprofit in order to give Ken every opportunity to regain past performance levels.

Firing Ken to maximize performance without regard to his interests is using an end justifies the means approach to decision making. But to treat a person as an end is to respect that person's dignity by allowing them the freedom to make their own choices.[199] This point argues for keeping Ken on and at least allowing him the opportunity to recover to a level of performance previously reached.

Check Yourself and Behave Ethically

How would you feel if your decision was widely discussed in the organization? Could you defend it in good conscience? Would morale suffer if Ken were fired? We can imagine all kinds of negative comments by those in the AIDS community about the firing. As the manager, you should be prepared to address their concerns.

As with most ethical dilemmas, there's no easy answer. Considering how you would feel or react if the decision was discussed on social media provides an opportunity for a "gut check"—an honest, reflective appraisal of the intended action.

It's always a good idea to think outside the box and consider alternative ways of handling an ethical dilemma. For example, if you decide to fire Ken, then perhaps he could be given a good severance package with health benefits. Alternatively, perhaps Ken can be moved to another position where fund-raising is not required and his talents can be used for the betterment of the nonprofit and its constituents.

Should Parents Monitor Teens' Social Media Activities?

Teens spend on average of eight hours per day online. Their online behaviors have implications for their health and well-being. It's important to set the ground rules when you as a parent first give a smartphone, tablet, computer, or other electronic device to a teen, including that they will be monitored until they are old enough to understand their obligations online. You can open up more features as the teen demonstrates their ability to follow the rules, meet your expectations, and understand the consequences of unacceptable behaviors.[200]

The extent to which parents should monitor their teens' social media activities is a question every parent faces. Most parents monitor their teens' activities on social media. A survey by the Pew Research Center in 2014–2015 provides the following information.[201]

Do parents talk to their kids about acceptable online behavior? The results are the combined scores for parents' answers of *frequently* and *occasionally*:

Activity	Score
Behavior in their schools, home, and social lives	89%
Content to share online	82%
Content for them to be viewing online	79%
Content to consume via TV, music, books, magazines, other media	79%
Online behavior toward others	78%

These kinds of discussions can provide important benefits by helping to instill ethical behavior in teens. It's also important to have these discussions to protect their safety and security, basic needs in Maslow's model. Teens may unknowingly become involved in potentially dangerous behaviors online through chat rooms, instant messaging, and emails. Predatory behavior can have damaging effects on a teen's self-image and feelings of self-worth. It's important to have conversations with teens to be sure they're aware of the warning signs and what to do when they feel a predator is in their midst.

Another reason to monitor teens' online activities is to teach them about cyberbullying. Cyberbullying manifests in name-calling or insults, spreading gossip and rumors, and circulating unflattering pictures. Cyberbullying threatens the safety and security of teens. It can create harmful effects, including hurt feelings, sadness, depression, anxiety, anger, shame, fear, frustration, low self-esteem, inability to trust others, withdrawal, avoidance of social relationships, poor academic performance, bullying of others, and, in extreme cases, suicide.[202] Being targeted online can destroy feelings of self-worth and make it virtually impossible to self-actualize. These behaviors make it more difficult for a teen to be happy and lead a meaningful life.

Consequentialism

Arguments for Monitoring

- Communicating with a teen about social media limitations can build responsible behavior and they learn to be accountable for their actions.

- Monitoring their behavior can help deal with problems such as sexting and cyberbullying that can be harmful to their growth and development.

- Monitoring can help to control for predatory behavior that threatens a teen's well-being.

- Discussing online behaviors can be used as a teachable moment to explain what's meant by respecting others and how online behaviors promote civility in relationships.

Arguments against Monitoring

- Teens have a right to privacy and may not want their parents to see everything they do on social networking sites; they may perceive it to be invading their sacred online space.

- Trusting parents is a key issue in strengthening the bond between teen and parent.

- Teens may wonder what else parents are monitoring; do they follow them on dates, for example, especially at younger ages?

Returning to the original question: Should parents monitor teens' online activities? If you are a parent, the benefits of doing so and protecting your kids against harmful behaviors outweighs the costs. Yes, privacy and trust are important issues to teens, and they may not understand why you have chosen to ignore these. Still, you are the parent and should provide guidance for your teen in navigating the sometimes choppy waters online. Ask yourself: How would you feel if you didn't monitor those activities and your teen became the target of a predator or was cyberbullied?

Should You Put an Aging Parent in an Assisted Living Facility?

Your mother is eighty years old and basically in good health. Your dad died several months ago and, as the only child, the responsibility of caring for your mom has fallen on your shoulders. The first couple of months were fine, but, increasingly, your mother has become demanding—asking you to make more time to take her to doctor appointments, luncheons with friends, and so forth.

It's hard for you because you work full-time and like to visit your grandchildren, who live in another state, whenever you can. At first, you hired a home care nurse because there is a spare room in the basement of your mother's house. It didn't work out well. Your mom didn't like a stranger in the house and claimed the home care person stole from her.

You're losing patience and are considering putting her in an assisted living facility just two miles from your home. You can visit most days after work and on weekends and take your mom out for a meal or a movie. You have the money to pay for the care, but, over time, it may put a dent in your savings and limit your ability to do fun things.

What are the ethical issues of concern in deciding what to do?

There are many practical considerations, some of which would depend on the circumstances of each case. Is there a moral obligation to take care of an aging parent? Undoubtedly, there are different views on this issue. More to the point, there is a moral obligation to ensure the care of a parent is the best it can be.

Arguments for Putting Mom in Assisted Living

- Mom can get the 24/7 care she needs.

- Medical personnel are on site or just a phone call away, so she'll be cared for if an illness or other infirmity occurs.

- Someone will make sure she takes her medications on schedule.

- The meals at the facility are nutritious; she'll eat regularly.

- She'll be exposed to many activities appropriate for her age.

- A physical therapist comes in once a week to work with the patients on light exercises.

- A burden is lifted from your shoulders and you can go about living your life, including visiting your grandkids more often.

Arguments for Taking Care of Mom Yourself

- It's a money saver.

- You can take her with you to visit the grandkids.

- You can get temporary care when necessary.

- It alleviates your concern about whether she'll fit in at the assisted living facility, make new friends, won't be lonely.

- It alleviates your concern that Mom will not be able to maintain her longstanding friendships outside the facility.

- It mitigates the feeling that you will have betrayed your mother if you put her in assisted living.

How does each alternative affect your mom's well-being? It's difficult to say because each case is personal and different priorities exist. Still, it's clear that any analysis should incorporate ethical values such as compassion, empathy, and personal responsibility. We could assume that Mom would be happier at home, in familiar surroundings, closer to you, where she is able to keep up with her friends. On the other hand, many elderly people do quite well in assisted living, especially if they have good socialization skills. She can make new friends, perhaps ones closer to her age and with similar health and medical concerns. Either way, your goal should be to make sure your mom gets the care she needs. The ends of providing the best care possible exceed the costs that may be incurred to achieve that result, although you do not have an obligation to put her in assisted living if it creates too much of a financial strain.

An important question in deontology is about your intentions in taking care of Mom yourself or putting her in assisted living. If it is inconvenient to care for her in your home, you don't have the time or inclination, or you simply don't want to be bothered, then your motivation for putting her in assisted living is self-serving. If, on the other hand, you truly believe the assisted living care will be better for her— maybe you don't cook meals or you come home too late to do so—then your motives are good ones. She may also thrive in a setting more suitable for her age. Remember to check yourself before deciding: Would you want your kids to put you in an assisted living facility when you reach the same stage of your life, assuming health, financial, and other considerations were similar?

Ethics Activities

Ethics in Personal Relationships

Often, we take loved ones for granted. We may fail to value their contribution to our lives. Our close, meaningful relationships with family and friends can create happiness for us and add greater meaning to our lives, which is why it's so important to understand the reciprocal effects of our interactions with them.

One way to improve the quality of those relationships is to understand how we add value to them and how they add value to us. Try the following activity to highlight how your important relationships add meaning to your life and how you can do the same for them.[203] This is a good technique if you're wondering whether to stay in a relationship.

What do they do for you?   What do you do for them?

_____   _____

_____   _____

_____   _____

_____   _____

_____   _____

_____   _____

Workplace Ethics

Each of us brings certain qualities to the workplace that can help us develop meaningful work relationships and pursue excellence in everything we do.[204] We need to be sure we get enough positive feelings from work that enable us to reach our higher levels of need: esteem/feelings of self-worth and self-actualization. It's important to understand what you bring to the workplace and what it provides for you.

Values you bring to   Emotional feelings
the workplace   generated from work

_____   _____

_____   _____

_____   _____

_____   _____

_____   _____

_____   _____

Online Behaviors

Our online behaviors can enhance our well-being or bring harm to us. Think about things you do online that bring happiness and add meaning to your life and those that might have the opposite effect.

Enhances well-being   Not beneficial to well-being

_____   _____

_____   _____

_____   _____

_____   _____

_____   _____

_____   _____

Conclusion

We've reached the end of our journey. By now, you have a better understanding of what ethical behavior is and how acting ethically can bring happiness and greater meaning to your life. It's time to put these lessons to practice. As you engage in different relationships, keep notes about what you did, why you did it, what the outcome was, and what you would do differently if you face similar situations in the future.

We encounter new situations all the time. Our ethical behavior is always evolving. It's a dynamic process, but one that can benefit from using the decision-making process discussed in this book, which provides a structure to ensure you carefully think about your options, identify the key ethical values, weigh the consequences, consider your moral duties, and make the best ethical choice possible.

Committing to being an ethical person is not an easy task in a world where the pursuit of self-interest can blind us to ethical issues, a world where a lack of civility makes it more difficult to achieve happiness, an environment where our social networking activities can create obstacles to developing meaningful relationships.

We can, however, overcome these obstacles through ethical behavior and transform our lives for the better. It starts by treating others the way we wish they would treat us. It requires that we consider the possible consequences of our actions on others and what our moral duties are. We can make a difference in the quality of our own life and the lives of others by being virtuous, doing what is right because it is the right thing to do, and making decisions that are good, not bad. These are the ingredients of a life well lived.

Glossary

Altruism: Kind, selfless behavior often motivated by feelings of compassion.

Applied ethics: The application of moral reasoning to practical situations.

Boundedly ethical: Individuals who do not always recognize the ethical dimensions of their decisions because they are subject to ethical blind spots.

Bystander effect: When those who can change the outcome of an event stand back and do nothing, hoping or rationalizing that others will step forward instead.

Caring: Concern for the welfare of others by treating them with kindness and compassion and empathy.

Categorical imperative: An unconditional moral obligation that is not dependent on a person's inclination or purpose.

Catfishing: When someone pretends to be something they're not by using social media sites to create false identities, particularly to pursue deceptive online romances.

Character ethic: Covey's notion that we should align our values with universal and timeless principles such as fairness, integrity, honesty and truthfulness, and treating people with respect.

Citizenship: Includes civic virtues and duties that prescribe how we ought to behave as part of a community.

Civility: Polite, reasonable, and respectful behavior toward others.

Cognitive gap: A divide between a person's view of themselves as a good person and what they do that cannot be called good.

Compassion: Being concerned about the condition of others and feeling an emotional response to both their pain and pleasure.

Consequentialism: A form of ethical reasoning that morality is about making decisions that produce the best overall consequences.

Corporate culture: The shared beliefs of top managers in a company about how they should manage themselves and other employees, and how they should conduct their business(es).

Corporate governance: Systems in place to ensure a company is run properly and with an ethical corporate culture.

Cyberbullying: Willful and repeated harm inflicted by name-calling, spreading gossip and rumors, and circulating unflattering pictures on computers, cell phones, and other electronic devices.

Deontology: A form of ethical reasoning that emphasizes one's moral duties to others (Kantian ethics).

Descriptive ethics: A view of ethics from the perspective of how things have occurred and why.

Distributive justice: How benefits and burdens should be distributed among a group of people.

Egoism: The theory that one's self is, or should be, the motivation for all actions.

Empathy: Understanding another person's situation by seeing things through their eyes and being sensitive to their feelings.

Enlightened egoism: A type of egoism that allows for the well-being of others when that consideration helps achieve some ultimate goal of the decision maker, although the decision maker's own self-interest remains paramount.

Ethical action: Summoning up the courage to act ethically even in the face of countervailing forces.

Ethical awareness: The ability of an individual to recognize an ethical issue, problem, or dilemma.

Ethical blind spots: The gaps between who you would like to be and the person you truly are.

Ethical character: Possessing those qualities or characteristic traits of behavior called ethical values or virtues.

Ethical egoism: Claims that the promotion of one's own good is in accordance with morality and that personal happiness is regarded as intrinsically valuable insofar as it is pursued for its own sake and not the sake of others.

Ethical fading: Circumstances that arise where the ethical aspects of a decision disappear from view and the moral implications are obscured.

Ethical intent: Being motivated to do the right thing.

Ethical judgment: The ability to reason through ethical dilemmas and determine the best course of action.

Ethical principles: General judgments that serve as a justification for particular ethical prescriptions and evaluations of human actions.

Ethical relativism: There are no universal, permanent criteria to determine ethical behavior but variable ones that depend on the person, circumstances, or social situation.

Ethical sense: The result of practicing ethics through the choices we make, reasons for our choices, and the actions we take to carry through ethical intent with ethical action.

Ethical slippery slope: A pattern of behavior in which small unethical infractions lead to more egregious behaviors over time, which may lead to unintended consequences.

Ethics: The systematic and reasoned study of moral right and wrong, good and bad, including the principles and claims that employ these concepts.

Eudaimonic well-being: Achieving a sense of purpose by setting and reaching goals so that one's life is worthwhile.

Extrinsic value: Something that doesn't have intrinsic worth but is done for another reason such as external reward.

Fairness: A balanced standard of justice that addresses issues of equality, impartiality, and due process without relevance to one's own feelings, inclinations, and biases.

Fight-or-flight response: A physiological reaction that occurs in the presence of something that causes great fear, either mentally or physically, and uncertainty how best to respond to the threatening situation.

Formula of humanity: Humanity must always be treated as an end, not merely a means, and each person has a worth or dignity that must be respected.

Formula of universal law: The reasons for our actions should be those that, by virtue of being rational, everyone would act in precisely the same way.

Fraud: A willful act that violates the law with the intention of deceiving another party.

Ghosting: When someone you believe cares about you, such as a person you have been dating, disappears from contact without any explanation at all—no phone call, email, or text.

Ghosting in the workplace: When someone interviewing for a job does not follow through and inform prospective employers of their decision, and when employers decide not to offer employment to a candidate, who is not informed of that decision.

Golden Mean: An idea in virtue theory that extremes in behavior should be avoided and, instead, moderation of our actions would lead to virtuous behavior.

Golden Rule: An ethic of reciprocity that suggests we should treat others with the same consideration that we demand for ourselves.

Good will: A universal action is one that is good in every instance of occurrence and is motivated by good intentions.

Gratitude: Expressing appreciation for someone or something, which produces a more long-lasting positive feeling and builds stronger relationships.

Greatest Happiness Principle: Actions are considered moral when they promote happiness and avoid unhappiness; we should seek to maximize pleasure over pain.

Happiness: In Greek ethics of virtue, moral excellence and the end state of human flourishing.

Hedonic well-being: Achieving happiness by maximizing one's pleasurable moments: seeking pleasure, avoiding pain.

Honesty: Expressing the truth as best we know it and not conveying it in a way likely to mislead or deceive.

Human flourishing: Characterized by a life worth living, the good life, and a state of well-being.

Inside out: Covey's idea (*The 7 Habits of Highly Effective People*) that change starts from within in order to develop personal effectiveness and develop healthy relationships with other people.

Integrity: A character trait of a person with moral courage who is willing to stand up and do the right thing even if there are personal costs.

Intellectual virtues: Virtues that govern our thought process and that are acquired through understanding, good judgment, and practical wisdom, the end result of which is expressed in purposeful action.

Intrinsic value: Something that has value in its own right or for its own sake and that needs nothing outside itself to give it value.

Justice: Treating others fairly, equally, unless they are different in ways that are relevant to the situation in which they are involved.

Kill the messenger: Attitude of "don't blame me for some wrongdoing because I'm just the bearer of the bad news."

Kindness: A quality of being warm, generous, and considerate through concern for another and empathy.

Loyalty: A quality of being faithful to our obligations to others to promote their interests but in a way that doesn't harm others.

Maslow's hierarchy of needs: A motivational theory of human needs that progress from physiological and psychological needs to social needs, self-actualization, and transcendence.

Meaningful life: When our actions are worthwhile and are accompanied by a sense of value in our accomplishments, we can be said to lead a meaningful life.

Meaningfulness: Entails a value judgment, or a cluster of them, which in turn implies a certain kind of emotion.

Mental well-being: How well we can cope with day-to-day life.

Moral agent: A person who has the ability to distinguish between right and wrong and to be held accountable for their actions that should not cause unjust harm.

Moral courage: To act for moral reasons despite the risk of adverse consequences.

Moral muscle memory: An automatic response to a heightened emotional state that enables us to draw on past experiences to anticipate the arguments we may hear for unethical behavior.

Moral nihilism: Nietzsche's view that there is no absolute basis for right or wrong.

Moral virtues: Virtues that govern our behavior through traits such as temperance or self-control, courage, and justice.

Morals: What a person, group, or society believes people should or should not do that may be influenced by religious and cultural beliefs.

Motivated blindness: When it's in the best interests of the decision maker not to see the unethical behavior of others.

Normative ethics: A view of ethics from the perspective of how things ought to be, how to value them, which things are good or bad, and which actions are right or wrong.

Objectivism: A version of egoism that holds there is no greater moral goal than achieving happiness for oneself through the exercise of reason (Rand's rational egoism).

Office politics: The strategies people use to gain an advantage for themselves within a company or business.

Peak experiences: Highly valued experiences that are characterized by an intensity of perception, depth of feeling, and profound significance that they stand out in the subject's mind and transcend meeting our own needs to contributing to the betterment of others.

Physical well-being: Lifestyle behavior choices to ensure health, avoid preventable diseases and conditions, and live in a balanced state of mind and spirit.

Ponzi scheme: A fraudulent investing scam promising high rates of return with little risk to investors because it uses the funds of other investors.

Promise keeping: A commitment to do something that creates a legitimate basis for another person to rely upon us.

Rational egoism: Rand's claims that the promotion of one's own interest is always in accordance with reason and that an action is rational if and only if it maximizes one's self-interest.

Rationalizations (for unethical actions): Explanations we tell ourselves and others for improper behavior.

Reliability: Keeping promises and honoring commitments to others by accepting the responsibility of making all reasonable efforts to fulfill our commitments.

Respect: Treating people with dignity, courteously, and decency, not rudely, and holding them in high esteem.

Responsibility: Being accountable for what we do and what we say.

Rights theory: A normative ethics theory espoused by Kant that recognizes the existence of justified claims against others who have a duty to respect one's rights (i.e., autonomy, self-determination, and freedom).

Self-actualization: Reaching one's full potential and achieving a higher purpose in life.

Self-control: The presence of a strong will to self-regulate behavior (virtue ethics).

Self-deception: Being unaware of the processes that lead us to form our opinions and judgments, causing the avoidance of truth, lies that we tell ourselves, and secrets we keep from ourselves.

Self-esteem needs: Positive feelings of self-worth that arise from developing close relationships.

Selfish: Excessive or exclusive concern about oneself: seeking or concentrating on one's own pleasure or well-being without regard for others.

Self-ish: Being loving, kind, and caring toward yourself; honoring the commitments you make to yourself; and taking care of all aspects of yourself—body, mind, and spirit.

Self-transcendence: Focusing on things beyond the self, like altruism, spiritual awakening, liberation from self-interested behavior, and the unity of being that contribute to the betterment of society.

Sexting: Sending sexually explicit material, explicit photographs, or videos through text messages.

Sexual harassment: Actions that are unwanted and affect workplace ethics sometimes by creating a hostile work environment.

Situational ethics: A form of ethical relativism where right and wrong depend upon the facts of each situation rather than prescribed norms of behavior such as the Golden Rule.

Six Pillars of Character: The underlying ethical values identified by the Josephson Institute of Ethics that form the basis of moral duties and virtues.

Social responsibility: Ethical obligation of corporations and other entities to serve the best interests of stakeholders and advance the cause of ethics in society.

Stakeholders: Those affected by decisions, generally in the context of business decision making, including customers/clients, employees, top management, the entity, government, and the decision maker.

Subjective well-being: Scientific term for happiness and life satisfaction: thinking and feeling your life is going well, not badly.

Teleology: A form of ethical reasoning that explains an ethical decision by reference to some purpose, end, or goal.

Thriving: Experiencing a sense of development, of getting better at something, and succeeding at mastering something.

Tone at the top: The ethical environment that is created in the workplace by the organization's leadership and is expressed by standards of behavior incorporated into a code of ethics.

Transcendence: A level of development beyond self-actualization where we focus on the needs of others once our own needs have been satisfied.

Trolling on the internet: When a person starts quarrels or upsets people by posting inflammatory or off-topic comments online to provoke others.

Trustworthiness: Living up to the expectations of others and refraining from even small lies or self-serving behavior that can destroy relationships.

Truth telling: Being honest by expressing the facts as you know them without the omission of information, distortions, or white lies.

Utilitarianism: A form of consequentialism holds the best action is the one that maximizes the good and minimizes the bad by making a positive contribution to humanity.

Utility: A teleological principle described by Jeremy Bentham and John Stuart Mill that states actions or behaviors are right insofar as they promote happiness or pleasure, wrong if they tend to produce unhappiness or pain.

Values: Basic and fundamental beliefs that guide our actions and represent the intention behind purposeful action.

Virtue: A trait or quality that is deemed morally good and that becomes an excellence of character through practice and repetition (virtue ethics). The strength or will to fulfill one's duties despite any opposing inclinations (Kantian ethics).

Virtue ethics: A character-based approach to ethics of the ancient Greeks, including Aristotle, that assumes we acquire virtues through practice.

Virtuous character: An excellence of character that is concerned with choice and that is a mean between two extremes of behavior—excess and deficiency—this being determined by the way a person of practical wisdom would reason.

Well-being: Characterized by the experience of health, happiness, and prosperity that leads to good mental health, high life satisfaction, and a sense of purpose.

White lie: An untruth about a small or unimportant matter that someone tells to avoid hurting another person.

Workplace incivility: The exchange of seemingly inconsequential and inconsiderate words and deeds that violate conventional norms of workplace conduct.

Endnotes

1. E. Z. McGrath, *The Art of Ethics: A Psychology of Ethical Beliefs*, vol. 2., Values and Ethics Series (Chicago: Loyola University Press, 1994).

2. L. F. Thornton, "Civility Is an Ethical Issue," Leading in Context, August 8, 2012, https://leadingincontext.com/2012/08/08/ civility-is-an-ethical-issue/.

3. J. Vilhauer, "This Is Why Ghosting Hurts So Much…and Why It Says Nothing About Your Worthiness for Love," *Psychology Today*, November 27, 2015, https://www.psychologytoday. com/us/blog/living-forward/201511/is-why-ghosting-hurts- so-much.

4. M. Josephson, *Making Ethical Decisions*, ed. W. Hanson (Los Angeles: Josephson Institute of Ethics, 2002), https://store. charactercounts.org/wp-content/uploads/sites/10/2015/09/50- 0450-E.pdf.

5. "Introduction," Basics of Philosophy, accessed March 12, 2019, https://www.philosophybasics.com/branch_ethics.html.

6. J. Neusner and B. D. Chilton, eds., *The Golden Rule: The Ethics of Reciprocity in World Religions* (London: Continuum, 2009).

7. "Treat Others As You Want to Be Treated," Golden Rule, accessed March 12, 2019, http://www.harryhiker.com/goldrule. htm.

8. "Treat Others As You Want to Be Treated," http://www. harryhiker.com/goldrule.htm.

9. T. Irwin, *Nicomachean Ethics* (New York: Hackett, 1999).

10. N. S. Gill, "Timeline of Greek and Roman Philosophers," Thought Co., February 6, 2019, https://www.thoughtco.com/timeline-of-greek-and-roman-philosophers-118808.

11. The information in this exhibit is taken from two sources: S. M. Perdue, "The Big Three of Greek Philosophy: Socrates, Plato, and Aristotle," September 19, 2004, https://sites.psu.edu/rclperdue/2014/09/19/the-big-three-of-greek-philosophy-socrates-plato-and-aristotle/; and "Ancient Greek Philosophy," *Internet Encyclopedia of Philosophy*, https://www.iep.utm.edu/greekphi/.

12. R. C. Bartlett, *Nicomachean Ethics*, trans. S. D. Collins (Chicago: University of Chicago Press, 2012).

13. "Introduction: Aristotle's Definition of Happiness," Pursuit of Happiness, https://www.pursuit-of-happiness.org/history-of-happiness/aristotle/.

14. Bartlett, *Nicomachean Ethics*.

15. R. Burnor and Y. Raley, *Ethical Choices: An Introduction to Moral Philosophy with Cases* (New York: Oxford University Press, 2018).

16. M. Josephson, "Character—What Is It and Why Is It Important?" Josephson Institute of Ethics, http://josephsononbusinessethics.com/2015/02/character-what-is-it-and-why-is-it-important/.

17. Josephson Institute website, http://josephsoninstitute.org/michael-josephson/.

18. Josephson Institute of Ethics, *Making Ethical Decisions: The Six Pillars of Character* (Playa del Rey, CA: Josephson Institute of Ethics, n.d.), https://web.engr.uky.edu/~jrchee0/CE%20401/Josephson%20EDM/Making_Ethical_Decisions.pdf.

19. C. Sobczak, "Does Inequality Make Us Unhappy?" *Greater Good Magazine*, July 26, 2011, https://greatergood.berkeley.edu/article/item/does_inequality_make_us_unhappy.

20. E. Seppala, "Compassion Will Make You Happy," *Caring*, May 17, 2013, http://caringmagazine.org/compassion-will-make-you-happy/.

21. J. Locke, *An Essay Concerning Human Understanding*, ed. K. P. Winkler (Indianapolis, IN: Hackett Publishing, 1996).

22. "Calculating Consequences: The Utilitarian Approach to Ethics," Santa Clara University Markkula Center for Applied Ethics, https://www.scu.edu/ethics/ethics-resources/ethical-decision-making/calculating-consequences-the-utilitarian-approach/.

23. See *Internet Encyclopedia of Philosophy*, "Ethics," https://www.iep.utm.edu/ethics/; *Stanford Encyclopedia of Philosophy*, "Deontological Ethics," last updated October 17, 2016, https://plato.stanford.edu/entries/ethics-deontological/.

24. I. Kant, *The Groundwork for the Metaphysics of Morals*, 2nd ed., trans. M. Gregor and J. Timmermann (Cambridge: Cambridge University Press, 2012).

25. See *Internet Encyclopedia of Philosophy*, "Ethics," https://www.iep.utm.edu/ethics/; *Stanford Encyclopedia of Philosophy*, "Deontological Ethics," https://plato.stanford.edu/entries/ethics-deontological/.

26. O. C. Ferrell, J. Fraedrich, and L. Ferrell, *Business Ethics: Ethical Decision Making and Cases*, 11th ed. (Mason, OH: South-Western, Cengage Learning, 2011).

27. H. Sidgwick, *The Methods of Ethics* (Indianapolis, IN: Hackett Publishing, 1981).

28. *Stanford Encyclopedia of Philosophy*, "Egoism," last updated January 15, 2019, https://plato.stanford.edu/entries/egoism/.

29. E. Westacott, "What Is Ethical Egoism? Should I Always Pursue Only My Own Self-Interest?" *Thought Co.*, updated January 27, 2019, https://www.thoughtco.com/what-is-ethical-egoism-3573630.

30. C. Biddle, "The Beauty of Ayn Rand's Ethics," *Objective Standard*, December 28, 2010, https://www.theobjectivestandard. com/2010/12/the-beauty-of-ayn-rands-ethics/.

31. D. B. Rasmussen, "Rand on Obligation and Value," *Journal of Ayn Rand Studies* 42, no. 1 (Fall 2002): 69–86.

32. A. Rand, *The Virtue of Selfishness: A New Concept of Egoism* (New York: New American Library, 1964).

33. A. de Tocqueville, *Democracy in America* (Chicago: University of Chicago Press, 2000). (Original work published 1835)

34. R. F. White, "The Principle of Utility," http://faculty.msj.edu/ whiter/UTILITY.htm.

35. J. Troyer, ed., *The Classical Utilitarians: Bentham and Mill* (Indianapolis, IN: Hackett Publishing, 2003).

36. "Definition and Origines," Utilitarian Philosophy, http:// utilitarianphilosophy.com/definition.eng.html.

37. "Calculating Consequences: The Utilitarian Approach to Ethics," https://www.scu.edu/ethics/ethics-resources/ethical-decision-making/calculating-consequences-the-utilitarian-approach/.

38. T. Donaldson, P. H. Werhande, eds., with J. D. Van Zandt, *Ethical Issues in Business: A Philosophical Approach*, 8th ed. (Upper Saddle River, NJ: Prentice Hall, 2007).

39. *Internet Encyclopedia of Philosophy*, "John Stuart Mill: Ethics," https://www.iep.utm.edu/mill-eth/.

40. J. S. Mill, *Utilitarianism*, ed. George Sher (Indianapolis, IN: Hackett Publishing, 1979).

41. Mill, *Utilitarianism*.

42. M. Velasquez, C. Andre, T. Shanks, and M. J. Meyer, "Justice and Fairness," Santa Clara University Markkula Center for Applied Ethics, https://www.scu.edu/ethics/ethics-resources/ ethical-decision-making/justice-and-fairness/.

43. F. Nietzsche, *Basic Writings of Nietzsche*, trans. and ed. W. Kaufmann (New York: Modern Library Classics, 2000).

44. K. Mitcheson, "Sceptism and Self-Transformation in Nietzsche—on the Uses and Disadvantages of a Comparison to Pyrrhonian Scepticism," *British Journal for the History of Philosophy* 25, no. 1 (2017): 63–83.

45. *Stanford Encyclopedia of Philosophy*, "Intrinsic vs. Extrinsic Value," last updated January 29, 2019, https://plato.stanford.edu/entries/value-intrinsic-extrinsic/.

46. M. Velasquez, C. Andre, T. Shanks, and M. J. Meyer, "What Is Ethics?" Santa Clara University Markkula Center for Applied Ethics, https://www.scu.edu/ethics/ethics-resources/ethical-decision-making/what-is-ethics/.

47. M. Di Mento, "2017 Was a Banner Year, with 3 Gifts of $1 Billion or More," *Chronicle of Philanthropy*, January 2, 2018, https://www.philanthropy.com/article/2017-Was-a-Banner-Year-for-Big/242128?cid=cpfd_home.

48. J. R. Rest, "Morality," in *Handbook of Child Psychology: Cognitive Development*, vol. 3, series ed. P. H. Museen, and vol. ed. J. Flavell (New York: Wiley, 1983), 556–629.

49. Josephson Institute of Ethics, "Twelve Ethical Principles of Business Ethics," http://josephsononbusinessethics.com/2010/12/12-ethical-principles-for-business-executives/.

50. Saint Mary's College Institutional Review Board, "Basic Ethical Principles," https://www.stmarys-ca.edu/institutional-review-board/basic-ethical-principles.

51. D. Rottig, X. Koufteros, and F. Umphress, "Formal Infrastructure and Ethical Decision Making: An Empirical Investigation and Implications for Supply Management," *Decision Sciences* 42, no. 1 (2011): 163–204.

52. Vilhauer, "This Is Why Ghosting Hurts So Much," https://www.psychologytoday.com/us/blog/living-forward/201511/is-why-ghosting-hurts-so-much.

53. "POF Survey Reveals 80% of Millennials Have Benn Ghosted!" *Plenty of Fish Blog*, March 29, 2016, https://blog.pof.com/2016/03/pof-survey-reveals-80-millennials-ghosted/.

54. T. Shanks, "Everyday Ethics," Santa Clara University Markkula Center for Applied Ethics, https://www.scu.edu/ethics/ethics-resources/ethical-decision-making/everyday-ethics/.

55. T. Shanks, "Everyday Ethics," Markkula Center for Applied Research, https://www.scu.edu/ethics/ethics-resources/ethical-decision-making/everyday-ethics/.

56. E. Z. McGrath, *The Art of Ethics: A Psychology of Ethical Beliefs*, vol. 2, Values and Ethics Series (Chicago: Loyola University Press, 1994).

57. McGrath, *Art of Ethics*.

58. S. Mintz, "Why Do Ethical People Go Beyond the Law in Decision-Making?" Ethics Sage, December 8, 2015, https://www.ethicssage.com/2015/12/ethical-people-go-beyond-the-law-in-decision-making-laws-set-minimal-standards-of-behavior-many-people-make-the-mistake-of.html.

59. "Summary of Stephen R. Covey's *The 7 Habits of Highly Effective People*," QuickMBA, http://www.quickmba.com/mgmt/7hab/.

60. S. R. Covey, *The 7 Habits of Highly Effective People: Powerful Lessons in Personal Change* (New York: Free Press, 2004).

61. A. Hussain, "7 Habits of Highly Effective People (Book Summary)," HubSpot, https://blog.hubspot.com/sales/habits-of-highly-effective-people-summary.

62. Covey, *7 Habits of Highly Effective People*.

63. R. Sharma, "A Day of Listening," Robin Sharma, https://www.robinsharma.com/article/a-day-of-listening.

64. W. Phippen, "Nearly 400 People 'Pay It Forward' at St. Petersburg Starbucks," *Tampa Bay Times*, August 20, 2014, http://www.tampabay.com/news/humaninterest/more-than-250-have-paid-it-forward-at-local-starbucks-and-the-chain-is/2193784.

65. "What Is Moral Courage?" Lion's Whiskers, http://www.lionswhiskers.com/2011/02/what-is-moral-courage.html.

66. "Moral Courage," Definitions, https://www.definitions.net/definition/moral+courage.

67. L. F. Thornton, "'Ethics' Means Acting Beyond Self-Interest," Leading in Context, November 7, 2012, https://leadingincontext. com/2012/11/07/ethics-means-acting-beyond-self-interest/.

68. T. Ben-Shahar, "Self-Interest and Benevolence," Wholebeing Institute, https://wholebeinginstitute.com/self-interest-and-benevolence/.

69. "The Power of Moral Muscle Memory," Notre Dame Deloitte Center for Ethical Leadership, September 29, 2018, https:// ethicalleadership.nd.edu/news/lessons-on-developing-values-driven-leadership-from-mary-gentile-creator-director-of-giving-voice-to-values-video/.

70. "Do the Ends Justify the Means?" Got Questions, https://www. gotquestions.org/ends-justify-means.html.

71. S. Mintz, "What Is Civility?" Ethics Sage, April 2, 2012, https:// www.ethicssage.com/2012/04/what-is-civility-lack-of-respect-is-the-root-of-cause-of-incivility-the-word-civility-shares-an-etymological-root-wi.html.

72. "What Is Civility?" Institute for Civility in Government, https:// www.instituteforcivility.org/who-we-are/what-is-civility/.

73. J. C. Davis, "Civility and Its Discontents: Why Our Public Political Behavior Matters As Much As Ever," New York Daily News, June 29, 2018, http://www.nydailynews.com/opinion/ ny-oped-why-civility-matters-20180628-story.html.

74. "What Is Civility?" https://www.instituteforcivility.org/who-we-are/what-is-civility/.

75. T. G. Plante, "Is Civility Dead in America? Psychology Today, July 11, 2016, https://www.psychologytoday.com/us/blog/ do-the-right-thing/201607/is-civility-dead-in-america.

76. W. Shandwick and P. Tate, Civility in America 2018: Civility at Work and in Our Public Squares, 2018, https//www. webershandwick.com/wp-content/uploads/2018/06/Civility-in-America-VII-FINAL.pdf.

77. J. M. Jones, "More U.S. College Students Say Campus Climate Deters Speech," Gallup, March 11, 2018, https://news.gallup.

com/poll/229085/college-students-say-campus-climate-deters-speech.aspx.

78. L. F. Thornton, "Is Needing to Be 'Right' Unethical?" Leading in Context, September 5, 2012, https://leadingincontext. com/2012/09/05/is-needing-to-be-right-unethical/.

79. K. Jackson, "The Art of Selfishness: It's Not What You Think," SelfGrowth.com, https://www.selfgrowth.com/articles/The_ Art_of_Selfishness_It_s_Not_What_You_Think.html.

80. J. Fletcher, Moral Responsibility: Situation Ethics at Work (London: Westminster Press, 1967).

81. C. Porath and C. Pearson, "The Price of Incivility," Harvard Business Review, January–February 2013, https://hbr.org/2013/ 01/the-price-of-incivility.

82. D. Berenbaum, "Workplace Incivility on the Rise: Four Ways to Stop It," HR Exchange Network, March 23, 2010, https:// www.hrexchangenetwork.com/hr-talent-management/articles/ workplace-incivility-on-the-rise-four-ways-to-stop.

83. Berenbaum, "Workplace Incivility on the Rise," https://www. hrexchangenetwork.com/hr-talent-management/articles/ workplace-incivility-on-the-rise-four-ways-to-stop.

84. S. Lim, L. Cortina, and V. J. Magley, "Personal and Workgroup Incivility: Impact on Work and Health Outcomes," Journal of Applied Psychology 93, no. 1 (2008): 95–107.

85. The following discussion of biases comes from O. Sezer, F. Gino, and M. Bazerman, "Ethical Blind Spots: Explaining Unintentional Unethical Behavior," Current Opinion in Psychology 6 (2015): 77–81.

86. M. H. Bazerman and A. E. Tenbrunsel, Blind Spots: Why We Fail to Do What's Rights and What to Do About It (Princeton, NJ: Princeton University Press, 2011).

87. Sezer, Gino, and Bazerman, "Ethical Blind Spots."

88. S. Chapla, "Consider Yourself Ethical? New Research Says Think Again," Notre Dame News, July 12, 2011, https://news.

nd.edu/news/consider-yourself-ethical-think-again-says-new-research/.

89. S. Mintz and R. Morris, *Ethical Obligations and Decision Making in Accounting: Text and Cases,* 4th ed. (New York: McGraw-Hill Education, 2016).

90. K. Duggan, "Ethical Blind Spots: How to Minimize Their Impact," International City/County Management Association, March 27, 2018, https://icma.org/articles/pm-magazine/ethical-blind-spots.

91. Sezer, Gino, and Bazerman, "Ethical Blind Spots."

92. A. E. Tenbrunsel and D. M. Messick, "Ethical Fading: The Role of Self-Deception in Unethical Behavior," *Social Justice Research* 17, no. 2 (June 2004): 223–236.

93. S. Bok, *Secrets: On the Ethics of Concealment and Revelation* (New York: Vintage Books, 1989).

94. C. MacDonald, "What's Legal Isn't Always Ethical," Business Ethics Blog, December 11, 2011, https://businessethicsblog.com/2011/12/22/whats-legal-isnt-always-ethical/.

95. W. Wang, "Who Cheats More? The Demographics of Infidelity in America," Institute for Family Studies, January 10, 2018, https://ifstudies.org/blog/who-cheats-more-the-demographics-of-cheating-in-america.

96. "The Power of Moral Muscle Memory," https://ethicalleadership.nd.edu/news/lessons-on-developing-values-driven-leadership-from-mary-gentile-creator-director-of-giving-voice-to-values-video/.

97. B. Murphy, "Fallen Junk Bond King Milken Receives 10 Years in Jail," UPI, November 21, 1990, https://www.upi.com/Archives/1990/11/21/Fallen-junk-bond-king-Milken-receives-10-years-in-jail/3134659163600/.

98. C. Daniels, "The Man Who Changed Medicine," *Fortune,* November 29, 2004, http://archive.fortune.com/magazines/fortune/fortune_archive/2004/11/29/8192713/index.htm.

99. W. D. Cohan, "Michael Milken Invented the Modern Junk Bond, Went to Prison, and Then Became One of the Most Respected People on Wall Street," UPI, May 2, 2017, https://www.upi.com/Archives/1990/11/21/Fallen-junk-bond-king-Milken-receives-10-years-in-jail/3134659163600/.

100. C. K. Park, D. H. Lim, and B. Ju, "Transformational Leadership and Teacher Engagement in an International Context," in *Handbook of Research on Global Issues in Next-Generation Teacher Education*, ed. J. Keengwe, J. G. Mbae, and G. Onchwari (Hershey, PA: Information Science Reference, 2016).

101. E. Diener, "Subjective Well-Being," in *The Science of Well-Being: The Collected Works of Ed Diener*, vol. 1, ed. E. Diener (New York: Springer, 2009), 11–58.

102. I. Boniwell, "What Is Eudaimonia? The Concept of Eudaimonic Well-Being and Happiness," November 7, 2018, http://positivepsychology.org.uk/the-concept-of-eudaimonic-well-being/.

103. L. W. Henderson and T. Knight, "Integrating the Hedonic and Eudaimonic Perspectives to More Comprehensively Understand Wellbeing and Pathways to Wellbeing," *International Journal of Wellbeing* 2, no. 3 (2012).

104. T. Davis, "What Is Well-Being? Definition. Types, and Well-Being Skills," *Psychology Today*, January 2, 2019, https://www.psychologytoday.com/us/blog/click-here-happiness/201901/what-is-well-being-definition-types-and-well-being-skills.

105. Davis, "What Is Well-Being?" https://www.psychologytoday.com/us/blog/click-here-happiness/201901/what-is-well-being-definition-types-and-well-being-skills.

106. Mind.org, "How to Improve Your Mental Wellbeing," https://www.mind.org.uk/information-support/tips-for-everyday-living/wellbeing/#.W3MTU-hKjIU.

107. PPP Editorial Team, "What Is Gratitude and Why Is It So Important?" Positive Psychology Program, last updated February 14, 2019, https://positivepsychologyprogram.com/gratitude-appreciation/.

108. C. Ryff, "Happiness Is Everything, or Is It? Explorations on the Meaning of Psychological Well-Being," *Journal of Personality and Social Psychology* 57, no. 6 (1989): 1069–1081.

109. M. Seligman, *Flourish: A Visionary New Understanding of Happiness and Well-Being* (New York: Free Press, 2011).

110. E. Diener, S. Oishi, and R. E. Lucas. "Subjective Well-Being: The Science of Happiness and Life Satisfaction," in *Handbook of Positive Psychology*, ed. C. R. Snyder and S. J. Lopez (New York: Oxford University Press, 2002).

111. E. Diener, E. Sandvik, and W. Pavot, "Happiness Is the Frequency, Not the Intensity, of Positive versus Negative Affect," in *International Series in Experimental Social Psychology*, Vol. 21: *Subjective Well-Being: An Interdisciplinary Perspective*, ed. F. Strack, M. Argyle, and N. Schwartz (Elmsford, NY: Pergamon Press, 1991), 119–139.

112. Joaquín, "What Is Self-Actualization: A Psychologist's Definition [+ Examples]," Positive Psychology Program, modified 2018, https://positivepsychologyprogram.com/self-actualization/.

113. R. M. Niemiec, "Seven Pathways to Thriving," *Psychology Today*, November 8, 2017, https://www.psychologytoday.com/us/blog/what-matters-most/201711/seven-pathways-thriving.

114. D. J. Brown, R. Arnold, D. Fletcher, and M. Standage, "Human Thriving: A Conceptual Debate and Literature Review," *European Psychologist* 22, no. 3 (2017), https://econtent.hogrefe.com/doi/pdf/10.1027/1016-9040/a000294.

115. B. C. Feeney and N. L. Collins, "Thriving through Relationships," *Current Opinions in Psychology* 1 (February 1, 2015): 22–28, https://www.ncbi.nlm.nih.gov/pmc/articles/PMC4356946/pdf/nihms657382.pdf.

116. D. Nenninger and N. Nenninger, "20 Ways to Thrive in Life and Not Just Survive," *Port Jefferson, NY, Patch*, April 19, 2012, https://patch.com/new-york/portjefferson/amp/5647639/20-ways-to-thrive-in-life-and-not-just-survive.

117. R. Bronson, "The Relationship between Happiness and Well-Being," Thrive Global, September 4, 2018, https://thriveglobal.com/stories/the-relationship-between-happiness-and-wellbeing/.

118. His Holiness the Dalai Lama and H. C. Cutler, *The Art of Happiness*, 10th Anniversary Edition (New York: Riverhead Books, 2009).

119. His Holiness the 14th Dalai Lama of Tibet, "Brief Biography," https://www.dalailama.com/the-dalai-lama/biography-and-daily-life/brief-biography.

120. B. Schiller, "America, Desperate for Happiness, Is Getting Less and Less Happy," *Fast Company*, March 16, 2018, https://www.fastcompany.com/40544341/america-desperate-for-happiness-is-getting-less-and-less-happy.

121. *World Happiness Report 2019*, March 20, 2019, http://worldhappiness.report/ed/2019/.

122. J. Dorfman, "Sorry Bernie Bros but Nordic Countries Are Not Socialist," *Forbes*, July 8, 2018, https://www.forbes.com/sites/jeffreydorfman/2018/07/08/sorry-bernie-bros-but-nordic-countries-are-not-socialist/#183062ab74ad.

123. Devon McDermott quoted in W. R. Gould, "A White Lie Is a Bigger Deal Than You Think—and There's a Right and Wrong Time to Use One," *Business Insider*, June 21, 2016, https://www.businessinsider.com/the-right-and-wrong-time-to-use-a-white-lie-2016-6.

124. Gould, "A White Lie Is a Bigger Deal," https://www.businessinsider.com/the-right-and-wrong-time-to-use-a-white-lie-2016-6.

125. Josephson Institute of Ethics, "Six Pillars of Character," https://charactercounts.org/program-overview/six-pillars/.

126. M. Gielan, "Why Keeping Your Promise Is Good for You," *Psychology Today*, May 12, 2010, https://www.psychologytoday.com/us/blog/lights-camera-happiness/201005/why-keeping-your-promise-is-good-you.

127. K. Hall, "The Importance of Kindness," *Psychology Today*, December 4, 2017, https://www.psychologytoday.com/us/blog/pieces-mind/201712/the-importance-kindness.

128. E. E. Smith, "Masters of Love," *The Atlantic*, June 12, 2014, https://www.theatlantic.com/health/archive/2014/06/happily-ever-after/372573/.

129. Smith, "Masters of Love," https://www.theatlantic.com/health/archive/2014/06/happily-ever-after/372573/. See also L. C. Johnson, "Inside the Love Lab: Seven Principles of Making Marriage Work," *Positive Psychology News*, October 24, 2009, https://positivepsychologynews.com/news/laura-lc-johnson/200910244255.

130. "The True Meaning of Kindness," Becoming Who You Are, http://www.becomingwhoyouare.net/the-true-meaning-of-kindness/.

131. From C. Strauss and W. Kuyken, "What Is Compassion and How Can We Measure It? A Review of Definitions and Measures," *Clinical Psychology Review* 47 (May 2016): 15–27. See also J. L. Goetz, D. Keltner, and E. Simon-Thomas, "Compassion: An Evolutionary Analysis and Empirical Review," *Psychological Bulletin* 136, no. 3 (2009): 351–374.

132. B. Bland, "The Charter of Compassion," *Quest* 98, no. 3 (Summer 2010): 86.

133. "What Is Compassion?" *Greater Good Magazine*, https://greatergood.berkeley.edu/topic/compassion/definition.

134. E. M. Seppälä, "Compassion: Our First Instinct," *Psychology Today*, June 3, 2013, https://www.psychologytoday.com/us/blog/feeling-it/201306/compassion-our-first-instinct.

135. J. Stuart, "What Stops Us from Being Happy?" Project Happiness, https://shop.projecthappiness.org/blogs/project-happiness/what-stops-us-from-being-happy-1.

136. Cyberbullying Research Center, "What Is Cyberbullying?" https://cyberbullying.org/what-is-cyberbullying.

137. S. Pappas, "Social Media Cyber Bullying Linked to Teen Depression," *Scientific American*, June 23, 2015, https://www. scientificamerican.com/article/social-media-cyber-bullying-linked-to-teen-depression/.

138. L. Brown, "New Harvard Study Shows Why Social Media Is So Addictive for Many," WTWH Media, May 11, 2012, http:// marketing.wtwhmedia.com/new-harvard-study-shows-why-social-media-is-so-addictive-for-many/.

139. H. B. Shakya and N. A. Christakis, "A New, More Rigorous Study Confirms: The More You Use Facebook, the Worse You Feel," *Harvard Business Review*, April 10, 2017, https://hbr. org/2017/04/a-new-more-rigorous-study-confirms-the-more-you-use-facebook-the-worse-you-feel.

140. Park, Lim, and Ju, "Transformational Leadership and Teacher Engagement."

141. P. T. P. Wong, *The Human Quest for Meaning: Theories, Research, and Applications (Personality and Clinical Psychology)*, 2nd ed. (London: Routledge, 2012).

142. R. F. Baumeister, K. D. Vohs, J. L. Aaker, and E. N. Garbinsky, "Some Key Differences between a Happy Life and a Meaningful Life," *Journal of Positive Psychology* 8, no. 6 (2013).

143. R. Baumeister, *Meanings of Life*, rev. ed. (New York: Guilford Press, 1992).

144. E. E. Smith, *The Power of Meaning: Finding Fulfillment in a World Obsessed with Happiness* (New York: Broadway Books, 2017).

145. "Transforming the View on Asian Consumer Psychology," Martin Roll, July 2014, https://martinroll.com/resources/ articles/asia/transforming-view-asian-consumer-psychology/.

146. A. H. Maslow, "A Theory of Human Motivation" *Psychological Review* 50 (1943): 370–396.

147. The format and content of the model was taken from discussions about it in McLoed, "Maslow's Hierarchy of Needs," https:// www.simplypsychology.org/maslow.html. And "Maslow's Eight

Basic Needs and the Eight Stage Developmental Model," Mouse Trap, https://the-mouse-trap.com/2007/12/14/maslows-eight-basic-needs-and-the-eight-stage-devlopmental-model/. The title "Maslow's Motivation Model" better describes its purpose than the original "Hierarchy of Needs" because of the addition of three levels in the revised model.

148. D. Martin and K. Joomis, *Building Teachers: A Constructivist Approach to Introducing Education* (Belmont, CA: Wadsworth, 2007), 72–75.

149. A. H. Maslow, "A Theory of Human Motivation," *Psychological Review* 50, no. 4 (1943): 370–396; A. H. Maslow, *Motivation and Personality* (New York: Harper & Row, 1954).

150. McLoed, "Maslow's Hierarchy of Needs," https://www.simplypsychology.org/maslow.html.

151. A. H. Maslow, *The Farther Reaches of Human Nature* (London: Penguin Books, 2013).

152. McLoed, "Maslow's Hierarchy of Needs," https://www.simply psychology.org/maslow.html.

153. "Abraham Maslow," Pursuit of Happiness, http://www.pursuit-of-happiness.org/history-of-happiness/abraham-maslow/.

154. Leach, "Meaning and Correlates of Peak Experiences."

155. "Summary of Maslow on Self-Transcendence," Reason and Meaning, January 28, 2017, https://reasonandmeaning.com/2017/01/18/summary-of-maslow-on-self-transcendence/.

156. "What Is Self-Transcendence? Definition and 6 Examples," Positive Psychology Program, updated April 3, 2019, https://positivepsychologyprogram.com/self-transcendence/.

157. Martin and Joomis, *Building Teachers.*

158. C. Sperlazza, "Reasons to Get Out of Your Comfort Zone (And 10 Things You Can Do Right Now)," *Bulletproof Blog*, https://blog.bulletproof.com/step-outside-your-comfort-zone/.

159. J. Friedman, "Milton Friedman Was Wrong About Corporate Social Responsibility," *Huffington Post*, June 12, 2013, https://

www.huffingtonpost.com/john-friedman/milton-friedman-was-wrong_b_3417866.html.

160. A. Smith, *An Inquiry into the Nature and Causes of the Wealth of Nations*, ed. R. H. Campbell, A. S. Skinner, and W. B. Todd (Oxford: Oxford University Press, 1976). (Original work published 1776)

161. A. Smith, *The Theory of Moral Sentiments*, ed. D. D. Raphael and A. L. Macfie (Oxford: Oxford University Press, 1982). (Original work published 1759)

162. S. Fleischacker, "Adam Smith's Moral and Political Philosophy," *Stanford Encyclopedia of Philosophy*, Spring 2013 ed., https://plato.stanford.edu/entries/smith-moral-political/.

163. S. Mintz and R. Morris, *Ethical Obligations and Decision Making in Accounting: Text and Cases*, 5th ed. (New York: McGraw-Hill Education, 2020).

164. C. Caldwell, L. A. Hayes, and D. T. Long, "Leadership, Trustworthiness, and Ethical Stewardship," *Journal of Business Ethics* 96 (2010): 497–512.

165. A. Feldman and J. Kim, "The Hand Rule and the *United States v. Carroll Towing Co*. Reconsidered" (Working Paper No. 2002-27), https://www.econstor.eu/bitstream/10419/80224/1/363058788.pdf.

166. C. Leggett, "The Ford Pinto Case: The Valuation of Life As It Applies to the Negligent-Efficiency Argument" (manuscript, Spring 1999), https://users.wfu.edu/palmitar/Law&Valuation/Papers/1999/Leggett-pinto.html.

167. D. Birsch and J. Fiedler, eds., *The Ford Pinto Case: A Study in Applied Ethics, Business, and Technology*, SUNY Series, Case Studies in Applied Ethics, Technology, and Society (New York: SUNY Press, 1994).

168. *Grimshaw v. Ford Motor Co.* 119 Cal. App. 875 (1984), https://law.justia.com/cases/california/court-of-appeal/3d/119/757.html.

169. D. Shepardson, "Ford Agrees to $299.1 Million U.S. Takata Air Bag Settlement," Reuters, July 16, 2018, https://www.reuters.com/article/us-ford-motor-takata/ford-agrees-to-299-1-million-u-s-takata-air-bag-settlement-idUSKBN1K62JX.

170. H. Tabuchi and N. E. Boudette, "Automakers Knew of Takata Airbag Hazard for Years, Suit Says," *New York Times*, February 27, 2017, https://www.nytimes.com/2017/02/27/business/takata-airbags-automakers-class-action.html.

171. "Five Things to Know About VW's 'Dieselgate' Scandal," Phys.org, June 18, 2018, https://phys.org/news/2018-06-vw-dieselgate-scandal.html.

172. T. Leggett, "How VW Tried to Cover Up the Emissions Scandal," BBC News, May 5, 2018, https://www.bbc.com/news/business-44005844.

173. R. Parloff, "How VW Paid $25 Billion for 'Dieselgate'—and Got Off Easy," *Fortune*, February 6, 2018, http://fortune.com/2018/02/06/volkswagen-vw-emissions-scandal-penalties/.

174. The information in the Wells Fargo case comes from the following: M. Pastin, "The Surprise Ethics Lesson of Wells Fargo," January 20, 2017, https://www.huffingtonpost.com/mark-pastin/the-suprise-ethics-lesson_b_14041918.html; S. Mintz, "Navigating the Choppy Waters of Unethical Behavior at Wells Fargo," Ethics Sage, October 11, 2016, https://www.ethicssage.com/2016/10/navigating-the-choppy-waters-of-unethical-behavior-at-wells-fargo.html.

175. "Whistleblower: Wells Fargo Fraud 'Could Have Been Stopped,'" CBS News, August 3, 2018, https://www.cbsnews.com/news/whistleblower-wells-fargo-fraud-could-have-been-stopped/.

176. "The McDonald's Hot Coffee Case," Consumer Attorneys of California, https://www.caoc.org/?pg=facts.

177. "McDonald's Hot Coffee Case," https://www.caoc.org/?pg=facts.

178. "What Is a Ponzi Scheme?" Investopedia, https://www.investopedia.com/terms/p/ponzischeme.asp.

179. M. Assad, "Madoff Scam Still Cuts Local Victims," Morning Call, October 20, 2015, https://www.mcall.com/business/mc-bernie-madoff-victims-20151020-story.html.

180. C. Nobel, "Bernie Madoff Explains Himself," Harvard Business School Working Knowledge, October 24, 2016, https://hbswk.hbs.edu/item/bernie-madoff-explains-himself.

181. Nobel, "Bernie Madoff Explains Himself," https://hbswk.hbs.edu/item/bernie-madoff-explains-himself.

182. M. Brenner, "Whistleblower: The Man Who Knew Too Much," Vanity Fair, May 1996, https://www.vanityfair.com/magazine/1996/05/wigand199605.

183. C. Salter, "Jeffrey Wigand: The Whistleblower," Fast Company, April 30, 2002, https://www.fastcompany.com/65027/jeffrey-wigand-whistle-blower.

184. "Jeffrey Wigand on 60 Minutes, February 4, 1996," Jeffrey Wigand.com, http://www.jeffreywigand.com/60minutes.php.

185. E. MacAskill and A. Hern, "Edward Snowden: 'The People Are Still Powerless, but Now They're Aware,'" The Guardian (Manchester), June 5, 2018, https://www.theguardian.com/us-news/2018/jun/04/edward-snowden-people-still-powerless-but-aware.

186. V. Xu, "Edward Snowden Talks Ethics of Whistleblowing," Stanford Daily, May 19, 2015, https://www.stanforddaily.com/2015/05/18/edward-snowden-talks-ethics-of-whistleblowing/.

187. S. Chayutworakan, "Cabbie Returns B300,000 in Lost Cash to American Tourist," Bangkok Post, December 5, 2018, https://www.bangkokpost.com/news/general/1588082/cabbie-returns-b300-000-in-lost-cash-to-american-tourist.

188. "Ethical Issue," Business Dictionary, http://www.businessdictionary.com/definition/ethical-issue.html.

189. M. Josephson, "Commentary 772.2: Ethics—Easier Said Than Done," Michael Josephson's What Will Matter (blog), Josephson Institute, http://whatwillmatter.com/2012/04/commentary-772-2-ethics-easier-said-than-done/.

190. P. Day, "How to Catch a Catfish, from Someone Who's Been There," *Newcastle Tab*, 2017, https://thetab.com/uk/newcastle/2017/02/03/catch-catfish-someone-whos-catfished-eight-times-23114.

191. In a survey about catfishing discussed in the article "The Truth About Lying in Online Dating Profiles," 81 percent of users lied in their profiles; 48.1 percent lied about their height; 59.7 percent lied about their weight; and 18.7 percent lied about their age. Because of the prevalence of the activity, there is an MTV show, *Catfish: The TV Show*, that explores the truths and lies of online dating. Each episode investigates whether or not the other participant in the virtual relationship is legitimate or if they are, in fact, a "catfish."

192. "On the Philosophy of Catfishing," Mindless Philosopher, December 21, 2012, https://themindlessphilosopher.wordpress.com/2012/12/21/on-the-philosophy-of-catfishing/.

193. "Office Romance Hits 10-Year Low, According to Career Builder's Annual Valentine's Day Survey," Career Builder, February 1, 2018, http://press.careerbuilder.com/2018-02-01-Office-Romance-Hits-10-Year-Low-According-to-CareerBuilders-Annual-Valentines-Day-Survey.

194. "Millennials More Likely to Be Smitten with Superiors, Co-Workers," Workplace Options, February 8, 2012, https://www.workplaceoptions.com/polls/millennials-more-likely-to-be-smitten-with-superiors-co-workers-2/.

195. K. Cherry, "How the Fight or Flight Response Works," Very Well Mind, September 21, 2018, https://www.verywellmind.com/what-is-the-fight-or-flight-response-2795194.

196. R. Baumeister, "Self-Control—the Moral Muscle," *The Psychologist*, February 2012, https://thepsychologist.bps.org.uk/volume-25/edition-2/self-control-%E2%80%93-moral-muscle.

197. The ADA covers people with a physical or mental impairment that substantially limits major life activities. A person with such a disability is covered if he or she is subject to a prohibited action due to an actual or perceived impairment. Someone

who is HIV-positive typically meets this definition because HIV substantially limits life activities, such as functions of the immune system. Someone who is subjected to a prohibited employment action, such as termination, should be able to show that that action was taken against him or her because of an actual or perceived impairment.

198. This example is from "Ethical Dilemma Examples," Your Dictionary, https://examples.yourdictionary.com/ethical-dilemma-examples.html.

199. "Ethical Dilemma Examples," https://examples.yourdictionary.com/ethical-dilemma-examples.html.

200. "Should Parents Monitor Their Children's Social Media?" Teensafe, May 15, 2017, https://www.teensafe.com/blog/parents-monitor-childrens-social-media/.

201. M. Anderson, "How Parents Talk to Teens About Acceptable Online Behavior," Pew Research Center, January 7, 2016, https://www.pewinternet.org/2016/01/07/how-parents-talk-to-teens-about-acceptable-online-behavior/.

202. "The Dangers of Cyberbullying," Pure Sight Online Child Safety, http://www.puresight.com/Cyberbullying/the-dangers-of-cyber-bullying.html.

203. These activities are from "Ethics in Daily Life," https://www.slideshare.net/indianeducation/ethics-in-daily-life-60033478.

204. These activities are from "Ethics in Daily Life," http://download.nos.org/srsec321newE/321-Lesson-2.pdf.

Made in United States
North Haven, CT
14 October 2022